The Auto Biography

Mark Wallington is the author of the bestselling travel books *500 Mile Walkies* and *Boogie up the River*, both of which became radio series. His first credit as a scriptwriter was for *Not the Nine O'Clock News*. He has also written two novels, which he later adapted for television: *The Missing Postman* and *Happy Birthday Shakespeare*. In 1997 *The Missing Postman* won the British Comedy Award for Best Comedy Drama.

In 2005 he published *The Day Job*, an account of his years as a jobbing gardener in north London. He has written a number of film scripts for television, including *Station Jim* in 2000, and *The Man Who Lost His Head*, in 2007, and in 2012 he wrote *The Uke of Wallington*, a BBC Radio 4 Book of the Week about his travels around Britain with a ukelele.

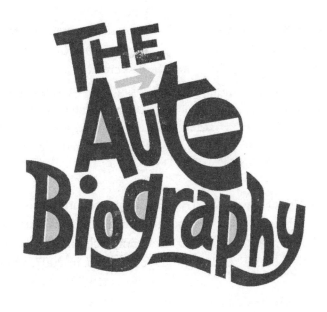

Mark Wallington

Published by AA Publishing, a trading name of AA Media
Limited, Fanum House, Basing View, Basingstoke, Hampshire,
RG21 4EA, UK.
www.theAA.com

First published in 2013
10 9 8 7 6 5 4 3 2 1

A CIP catalogue record for this book is available from the
British Library.

ISBN: 978-0-7495-7471-0

Cover design by Estuary English
Printed and bound by CPI Group (UK) Ltd, Croydon, CR0 4YY

A05017

Our books carrying the FSC label are printed on FSC certified
paper. FSC is the only forest certification scheme endorsed by the
leading environmental organizations.

MIX
Paper from
responsible sources
FSC® C018072

For BHW

CONTENTS

PART 1

HOME

Chapter 1

A Car is Born

This is how the story goes.

My father liked to check things on a car. He liked to check the oil and water, the brake fluid and battery levels. He liked to check the mileage. He loved to check tyre pressures and kept a little gauge with a pen clip inside his jacket pocket.

This would have been all very well had he owned a vehicle. But it was 1953, Britain was in post-war recovery, and while car ownership was no longer restricted to the wealthy, it was still considered an extravagance.

He would wait until neighbours bought one, then go round to admire it like a new baby. He'd ask about mpg and horsepower, ask them to lift the bonnet so he could inspect the engine. When they weren't looking he probably ducked down and took the tyre pressures.

Then one morning a tarmac spreader appeared at the top of our road, closely followed by a steam roller. By the time they reached the bottom, the old gravel had been buried forever. In its place was a rich, black, asphalt surface. My father could resist no longer. He said to my mother: 'It's time we bought a car.'

'Can we afford it?' she replied, busily knitting curtains. They already had one child, and I was on the way.

'We have a driveway. It's a waste not to use it.'

'Cars are nothing but traffic jams,' said my mother.

If a car was an extravagance so, it appeared, was a decent road network. Government investment was at a standstill; traffic jams grew up alongside car ownership like an annoying little brother. My father wasn't to be denied though: 'We've worked hard, damn it. We deserve to be in a traffic jam.'

'I'd rather have a television,' said my mother.

'A car will change our lives. We can have outings. We can visit Aunt Monica.'

'Next door they've got a car *and* a television.'

When my brother was born he was brought home from the maternity ward in a taxi, a Morris Cowley my father had logged in the birth book.

One taxi ride home with a newborn was enough. He was determined to have a car by the time I arrived. I was due the last week of May.

About 15,000 miles away in Nepal, John Hunt and his team had earmarked a similar date for the conquest of Everest. My father had followed their progress closely. 'Says here they've reached base camp,' he read to my mother from behind the newspaper.

'I reached base camp a long time ago,' she said. 'I'm near the summit.'

'We'll call the child John after John Hunt,' said my father.

'What if it's a girl?'

'We'll call him Hilary.'

My father became convinced I would be born on the day they climbed Everest. To have a new car delivered on the same date would be a fitting celebration. 'We should buy an Austin Everest really,' he said.

'Is there such a car?'

'No. They missed a trick there.'

They spent evenings carefully studying car brochures. Owing to the six-year halt in production during the war there was no second-hand market. There was even an embargo on selling cars within three years of purchase to stop profiteering. If you wanted a car you had to buy new.

'How about an Austin A30? It's got an 803cc engine and one windscreen wiper.'

'It's too... round,' said my mother.

'A Standard 8? Good pedigree vehicle. 803cc with one windscreen wiper.'

'Too oblong.'

She had eyes for the Ford Consul with its straight lines and white walled tyres. 'Very handsome,' she said.

My father didn't like the idea of anything so flash. The Consul was a car for wide boys. 'Beyond our budget,' he said. 'Two windscreen wipers for a start.'

'We'll ask what Grandma thinks,' said my mother.

'What's it got to do with her?'

'You'll be using the car to take her to the library.'

'She goes on the bus to the library.'

'What's the point in her spending money on a bus if you've got a car?' said my mother, carelessly planting the seeds of the monster that would, within a mere 50 years, lead to a dilapidated public transport system, an overloaded highway network, climate change, and the never-ending debate on whether wind farms are really worth the trouble.

My grandma had moved down from Manchester to join her daughter on the Dorset coast and bought the house next-door-but-one. She was a firm woman who had lived through two world wars with stoicism, and God had rewarded her with a television set nicely in time for the Coronation. She dusted it daily, and on top kept a picture of herself and her husband Frank on their wedding day. Whenever anyone called round she sat them down in front of the TV, even though there was rarely anything on except *Watch With Mother*.

'There's only one car worth buying,' said Grandma, 'and that's a Rolls-Royce.'

'Actually, Rolls-Royce isn't on the list,' my father pointed out.

'The Queen has a Rolls-Royce. Princess Margaret does too, and the Queen Mother.'

'We have to choose from these on the list.'

He showed her the pictures. She quickly pointed to the Ford Anglia.

'Why?'

'It's taller than the others.'

'What's tall got to do with it?' said my father. 'What does oblong or round have to do with it for that matter?'

'You can wear your hat in a tall car,' she said.

'You don't need to wear your hat in a car. That's what cars are for, so you can travel without a hat.'

Grandma shuffled at the idea of this. 'I think you'd be better off buying a television.'

'That's what I said,' said my mother.

My father decided to draw up a list of who drove what in town.

'We can't have a Humber, I'm afraid,' he said when my mother admired the doctor's Humber Hawk.

'Why not?'

'If we buy a Humber people will say, "Who does he think he is, a doctor?" It'll look as though I have ideas above my station.'

'How about a Vauxhall?'

'Can't have a Vauxhall either.'

'Mr Heath, the landlord at the Anchor, drives a Vauxhall.'

'Precisely. And he's divorced.'

This whole business was clearly more difficult than it appeared. My parents were learning what every motorist sooner or later learns: nothing says more about you than the car you drive.

'Oh, I don't care what sort of car we have,' said my mother.

'Saying you don't care what car you have is like saying, "I'm the kind of person who doesn't care about my image," which is an image in itself.'

My mother flicked through *Picture Post* to see what vehicles famous people drove.

'Max Bygraves drives a Bentley.'

'Well he would, wouldn't he?'

'David Niven drives an Alvis.'

'Yes, and General Montgomery drives a tank.'

The Everest team made camp on the South Col; two men suffered from frostbite. My mother made her camp on the sofa in the living room, suffering from cramps in the abdomen. Dr Armstrong came to examine her.

'I'd rather like the baby to be born on the day they climb Everest,' said my father.

'You need to speak John Hunt about that, not me,' said Dr Armstrong.

My father walked him out to his car. 'So, how do you find the Humber?'

'Good runner. Very comfortable.'

'How many windscreen wipers?'

'Two.'

'Luxury, eh?'

A week before my due date and my father was still undecided. He consulted Mr Besant who lived next door. The Besants were all redheads. They even had a ginger cat. They broke the cycle with their car though. It was a pale green Austin Devon.

My father told Mr Besant he was thinking of buying something similar, and asked to have a sit behind the wheel. 'Certainly,' said Mr Besant.

'Good mileage?' enquired my father.

'Excellent.'

'Use much oil?'

'Very little.'

'Is it true you've got a television as well?'

'Yes we have.'

The next day he came home from work looking very pleased with himself. He said to my mother: 'I've made our mind up.'

'What sort?'

'I'm not going to tell you. Except it's something special.'

The doctor came round again and decided my mother should go into hospital. 'She can't have the baby yet,' said my father.

'Why not?' asked Dr Armstrong.

'Because... the new car hasn't arrived,' although the real reason was because the Everest team had been held up by snow and ice.

'It's all right,' said Dr Armstrong. 'I can take her in.'

My father settled my mother into the broad back seat of the Humber. 'I'll pick you up in the new car, promise.'

But my father had no idea. Britain may have been the largest manufacturer of motor vehicles in Europe back then, but the government prioritized the lucrative export market, and 75 per cent of production went overseas. 'You mean British people have to wait until everyone else in the world has one of our cars?' my father complained down at the showroom.

Just as my mother went into labour, two members of the Everest team made an early attempt on the summit. My birth went without a hitch, but the climbers had to turn back due to lack of oxygen. Had they made it, my middle name would have been Everest.

My father felt let down. First the car and now this. 'Lack of oxygen, what sort of excuse is that?'

He had come to collect my mother and me from the maternity ward, but he was in a taxi.

'Where's the new car?' said my mother.

'It'll be here on the day they reach the summit.'

But they reached the summit and the car still didn't arrive.

'Don't worry. It'll be here for the Coronation.'

But Coronation Day dawned and there was still no sign of the new car. We all went over to Grandma's to watch the ceremony.

'It'll be here for the summer,' said my father, a little less convinced now. 'Perfect for picnics and outings to the New Forest.'

'Will it be here by June 21st?' said Grandma.

'Bound to be.'

'I'll get a fine if I don't have my library books back by then.'

In the end the new car didn't arrive until the autumn. My father went off to collect it. We lined up on the pavement outside the house and waited.

Then there he was, motoring smoothly up the hill in a shiny new vehicle that no one knew the name of.

'What is it?' asked my mother.

'It's a Ford Popular of course,' said my father.

'Never heard of it.'

'Well of course you haven't. It's a new model, just released.'

'What's so special about it?'

'It's the cheapest car in the world,' he whispered, so the neighbours couldn't hear.

'It's what?'

'The cheapest car in the world!' he yelled. Who cared what the neighbours thought?

This news did nothing but create an anti-climax. My mother squinted and said, 'What's so special about that?'

'It means we can buy a TV as well.'

The family joy knew no bounds. My grandma got taken to the library: 'I'm wearing a scarf instead of a hat, you'll notice.' My mother got to watch *Quatermass and the Pit*. And all five of us drove off on an outing and got stuck in a two-hour traffic jam on the A31, which pleased my father no end.

Chapter 2

The Cheapest Car in the World

The Ford Pop stood in the driveway like a biscuit tin on wheels. Because of the slope it was always left in gear with a chock in front of a back wheel. My father was not long out of the RAF and didn't trust anything so civilian as a handbrake.

'Nice colour, isn't it?' he said.

'Grey,' said my mother.

'Grey, but... a sort of delicate, misty grey.'

It was hard to compliment the Pop on its beauty or style. It was an upright vehicle that looked as though it hadn't been taken out of the box yet. Inside no discomfort had been spared: no carpet, no heater, low, rigid seats. The exterior hadn't troubled the designer much either, with bug-eyed headlights stuck on to the mudguards, a nose with large radiator nostrils, and no chrome. It was as if burglars had got to it before we did.

But what did you expect for £390? Plus a TV. The family certainly wasn't complaining; we were very proud. My mother furnished it to make it our own. There were no door pockets so she put a magazine rack in the gap between the seats. A ceramic ashtray was placed on the floor by the gear stick, large enough to contain my father's pipe and all its accessories. If there had been room she'd have put an occasional table with a vase of flowers in the back.

Whenever we went out for a drive it was classified as an outing and we dressed accordingly. My father wore a sports jacket and tie at the wheel during the week, an open shirt with cravat at the weekend. My mother wore make-up and heels. My brother and I both had our hair brushed and had to promise we'd been to the toilet. All this to go and buy the newspaper.

We were amateurs, though, compared to Grandma, who seemed to have to go to the library a lot more frequently.

'I need to change my book,' she'd say to my father.

'You changed it on Monday; you can't have read it already.'

'I got to page 12 and realized I'd read it before.'

Whenever he arranged to take her, she'd be ready half an hour early, sitting in her hallway in a coat, her handbag clasped on her lap, wearing the low-profile cloche hat with the emerald brooch she had designated her driving hat. My father would escort her to the car then hold open the door and she'd bend and duck and crash-land into the seat.

She used to shout in the car, whether the engine was running or not. 'Slow down, there's Mrs Coleman,' she'd yell, and knock on the window, then wave in a regal style.

The Ford Pop quickly became a family member, like the dog. Sunday was the children's bath day, and the car got a wash as well. My father would do the body and as we grew older we boys were given two wheels each. Then it was polished, and buffed. Every photo of us from those days includes the car, with my father standing with a hand resting on the bonnet like a concert pianist posing by his piano.

And, like a family member, the Pop had faults we had to learn to live with. 'Explain again why the windscreen wiper only works when you go downhill,' said my mother.

'Because it's vacuum powered,' said my father, with enough authority to disguise the fact that he didn't know what vacuum powered meant.

'I see,' said my mother, not wanting to admit she didn't know either. It was clear what it meant to us. It meant that the single windscreen wiper would go like a sewing machine if you were cruising down a hill, but would simply stop if you were going up one. 'Are you saying we can only go uphill in dry weather?' said my brother Andrew.

'Ssh, your father's driving,' said my mother.

There were no indicators on the Pop either. My father would wind the window down and stick his arm out and signal like a tic-tac man. This was nothing unusual, of course. The high street was full of drivers with their windows down communicating in a bizarre semaphore.

'The way a driver gives hand signals says a lot about him,' said my father.

'Like what?' said my mother.

'A good, firm, straight arm with a clearly defined loop indicates that a man with a decisive and confident nature is turning left. Whereas an arm hanging out of the window in a vague sort of flutter indicates...well, it probably indicates...' He chuckled and stopped.

'Indicates what?'

'Nothing...'

'You were going to say a woman driver, weren't you?'

'Of course not.'

My father drove us to school, then drove clients to view houses all morning, then drove home for lunch. 'Think of the money we're saving in bus fares and packed lunches,' he'd say to my mother as she put a hot meal on the table for him. It never occurred to him that motoring cost money. Anywhere he could drive he would do. The Pop was always willing.

Almost always. It didn't like the cold, and as it got older winters became a struggle. The starting handle usually did the trick, but the problem persisted to the point that my father visited the recently opened neighbourhood garage.

This was two pumps on the pavement and a workshop out back, and was run by Mr Goodall, who lived with his wife in a flat over the business. He wore a grey boiler suit and a beret and was trying hard to build up custom. There were bigger garages in town but his ploy was to keep his regulars happy. He rather overdid this though. He whistled while he worked, sang while he put petrol in.

'The sun has got his hat on,' he beamed as he cleaned the windscreen. 'Check your oil Mr Wallington?'

'No thank you,' said my father, who would never dream of letting anyone he didn't know near his dipstick.

'Tyres?'

'Tyres are perfectly fine.'

'Like to keep my regulars happy,' said Mr Goodall.

'One thing,' said my father, and explained the starting problem.

'Wet plugs,' said Mr Goodall. 'You have to dry them.'

'How?'

'Take them out and put them by the fire.'

Mr Goodall wasn't joking. So every morning the spark plugs were removed and put by the coal boiler in the kitchen. But this was a slow process. We needed to get to school, my father to work. We wiped the plugs down; blew on them; my father sat on them like a hen. Then my mother had the brainwave of putting them in the oven.

'Don't be ridiculous,' said my father.

'Why not? Fifteen minutes on Regulo 3 should do it.'

It became part of a winter morning's routine. My father would go out in his dressing gown and remove the spark plugs, then put them in the oven. The smell of breakfast on the stove would be offset by the piquant aroma of engine oil. He'd get dressed, replace the plugs and the engine would jump like a firecracker.

This was fun for a while, but soon became a chore. 'What we need of course,' he said, 'is overnight cover.' He glanced out of the kitchen window, and appeared to notice for the first time that both our neighbours had garages. 'Just a minute. Why haven't we got a garage!?'

In the same way as men always tried to repair their own cars in those days, they always had a go at building their own extensions as well. It would have been regarded as effeminate not to. And besides, a garage was nothing complicated.

'It's simple,' said my father.

'How simple?' said my mother, looking at the plans drawn on the side of a cereal box.

'Simple as making cement.'

Making cement was indeed simple, and we watched him as he made an awful lot of it, then poured it into a base. Around this he built a brick wall. He worked at it every weekend for six months. When he realized a garage was also going to need windows and a roof, he called in the prefabricated garage manufacturers. They arrived with all the materials in the morning and the job was done by the evening. From then on the Pop started just fine.

Motoring was fun and carefree and the government encouraged it because they could tax it so easily. So what if road safety was non–existent, and five thousand people a year got killed in car accidents?

We went on family picnics; we went to see Aunt Monica in Southampton. 'We fought the war for motoring,' said my father. When the rationing on bacon was finally lifted, victory was complete. 'Motoring and bacon, that's what we fought the war for.'

But he spoke too soon. In the summer of 1956 President Nasser of Egypt nationalized the Suez Canal. The British bombed Cairo and the Suez Crisis erupted. By the autumn there was a chronic shortage of oil.

'Petrol rationing's coming back,' announced Mr Goodall.

Within minutes a queue of traffic had formed at his pumps. Every adult could remember wartime fuel rationing, and if they knew one thing it was the importance of panic buying. My father filled up and then called at the butchers on the way home and bought a pile of bacon.

'Why?' said my mother.

'Petrol is just the start.'

The ration allowed the average car owner to travel 200 miles a month. My father stopped coming home for lunch. His beloved outings at the weekend had to end. Mr Norris from the tobacconist, who owned a bubble car that did 80 miles to the gallon, looked very smug.

'I bet the old Humber drinks the petrol,' said my father when Dr Armstrong called round – my mother was pregnant again.

'It's shocking,' said Dr Armstrong.

'You'll have to get a bike. Haha.'

'Haha,' said Dr Armstrong. 'Fortunately medical professionals are exempt from rationing.'

It turned out lots of professions were exempt. 'It says here, "religious ministers, farmers, midwives, veterinary surgeons". They're all exempt,' said my father from behind the paper. 'It's outrageous.'

'What's outrageous about it?' said my mother.

'If veterinary surgeons are exempt why can't estate agents be?'

'Doctors, ministers and farmers are essential services.'

He wanted to say, so are estate agents, but that was one step too far even for him.

From then on whenever he saw Dr Armstrong or the local vicar or any farmer driving round he'd say, 'I wonder where he's going? Probably the pub. Hardly essential.'

He became suspicious of anyone in a car. If they weren't exempt they must be dealing on the black market. Even neighbours were under suspicion. 'Mr Besant drives an awful lot if you ask me; he's just a teacher, he's not exempt. He must have a fiddle going.'

To gain exempt status became a quest. He sulked around the house until he came up with a plan. 'I think I should be exempt too,' he finally said to my mother.

'Why?'

'Because I need to take Grandma and her friends to the library and to the WI.'

'They'll happily take the bus.'

'Couldn't possibly have old ladies take the bus. One of them could fall, and then Dr Armstrong would have to come out and waste his fuel. No, I need to be exempt, not to the same degree as doctors and midwives perhaps, but certainly on a par with vets.'

'Well let's see what they say down at the Town Hall,' said my mother.

'I haven't got time for that lot.'

Now that he had convinced himself of his exempt status, the means by which he obtained the fuel didn't matter. Next time he went to Mr Goodall he was the one turning on the charm. 'The sun has got his hat on,' he sang.

Goodall looked at him oddly. 'What?' said my father.

When he handed over his petrol coupons he gave Goodall a two-bob tip.

'What's that?'

'A tip.'

'Are you after extra petrol or something?'

'No... well... I need to go and see Aunt Monica. She's got a bladder infection.'

This was more information than Mr Goodall needed. He cringed and sucked through his teeth.

'I always look after my regulars, Mr Wallington,' he said, and gave him a smile that implied: if I catch you buying petrol from any other garage, any time, for the next 30 years, or until I retire, whichever is later, then this will get in the *Western Gazette*.

He gave him half a tank. 'Give my best to Aunt Monica.'

With fuel my father was a happy man once again. 'Come on Grandma, we're going to the library.'

'I don't need to go to the library.'

'You're going to the library whether you like it or not.'

He took her to the library. He came home for lunch again. We went for a picnic. But then, as quickly as he went back to driving everywhere, he stopped and returned to the official rationing mileage.

'What was the point in all that?' said my mother.

'It's not really fair is it? I shouldn't be taking fuel away from vets. They do an important job.'

The truth was, I learned years later, he'd discovered a flaw in his plan. At the end of each week he would religiously record the Pop's mileage in its logbook. If he went over the 200-mile limit it would have been clear he'd obtained fuel unfairly.

He would have found this difficult to admit to, but not half as difficult as falsifying his logbook.

He fretted over this for a time. But there was no way round it. For that week he entered the correct figures in the log, but then in the margin under 'Comments' he added: 'Mileometer faulty, repair or replace.'

Chapter 3

The Brigitte Bardot of Motors

Every summer my mother's relations would come down from Lancashire for a summer break. Aunts Edith, Ethel and Gwen, and Uncles Jim and Harvey all came on the train. Only Uncle Michael, my mother's elder brother, drove. But Uncle Michael always did things differently. He was tall in an otherwise short family. He had a moustache while all the other men were clean-shaven. He lived in Birmingham. He was 30 but still single, and he smoked so much his index finger was brown with nicotine. He appeared so exotic it was hard to believe he was a member of our family. He even used to turn up in a different car each summer, that's how exciting he was.

'He's a bit showy, your brother is,' said my father.

'He's not showy, he's just fashionable,' said my mother.

'There's something a bit suspect about a man who changes his car every year.'

'You're just jealous.'

One year it would be a Ford Prefect, then a Corsair, then a Sunbeam Rapier with a convertible roof. He once showed up in an Austin Healey he said he'd borrowed from a friend.

'All his cars have fins and sharp bits,' said my father. 'He's become Americanized.'

It was 1960 and British vehicles had been heavily influenced by transatlantic design: their jelly mould physiques had been given straight lines; they'd grown tail-fins and wing mirrors and large back lights. The Ford Zephyr was the kind of car you could happily have taken to a drive-in movie.

Most things American were considered vulgar, but even my father had proved susceptible. The Ford Pop was showing its age. It began to leave a rust trail wherever it went; it leaked and made mad animal noises when you turned left. My father checked the oil one last time, then part exchanged it for a Hillman Minx.

'The Hillman has a fin,' said my mother.

'It's not a fin. It's a wing. There's a difference.'

That summer, rumour went round that Uncle Michael had bought something rather special, even for him. 'It'll be a Rolls-Royce,' said Grandma, who was still on a high after another royal TV event, the wedding of Princess Margaret and Antony Armstrong-Jones.

'If he's really been Americanized,' said my brother Andrew, 'then he'll be driving a Cadillac DeVille,' and he showed me a picture from our *Ladybird Book of Motor Cars*.

The other relatives arrived by train as usual. The aunts wore floral frocks and very red lipstick. The uncles had braces and spent the day sitting in deckchairs in Grandma's garden. The day Uncle Michael was due we all waited at the window to watch him arrive, pulling up in a very odd-looking white car.

'What is it?' said Uncle Harvey.

'It's a... It's a... I don't know,' said my father who, like the rest of us, was watching, transfixed, as the vehicle appeared to sit back as it came to a halt. We all looked to Andrew, who knew the name, model and cubic capacity of every car on the road.

'It's a Citroën,' said Andrew. 'A Citroën DS.'

There was a silence. 'You mean...it's foreign?' said my father.

'Where's it from?' asked my mother.

'France,' said Andrew.

'Ooh,' she said, and came over all girly as she ran out to greet Uncle Michael. '*Bonsoir, mon frère,*' she called.

'Typical,' said my father.

I'd never heard of Citroën. There weren't any in the Ladybird book and no one we knew in town had one. It wasn't British to look at, nor was it American. It didn't have pointy edges or round shoulders. It had sensual curves and a pout. 'Beauty, isn't she?' said Uncle Michael. 'I call her the Brigitte Bardot of motors.' And he tapped a Player's cigarette on the packet and lit it with his silver lighter.

The women fussed around it. Aunt Edith ran her finger over the bonnet. The men stood with their hands in their pockets, not getting too close, trying not to be impressed.

'It looks a bit like one of them bottom-feeding fish,' said Uncle Harvey.

'Designed by a sculptor, apparently,' said Uncle Michael.

'Antony Armstrong-Jones is a sculptor,' said Grandma.

'A photographer, mother.'

'A halibut,' said Uncle Harvey.

'What took you so long?' asked my father, trying to change the subject.

'Oh, I decided to go on the motorway,' said Michael.

This made even the men take a step back in shock.

'The motorway!'

'Yes. The M1.'

Now the men couldn't help but be impressed. Since the first section of the M1 had opened in Bedfordshire the previous year, my father had longed to have a drive on it.

'What was it like?' said Uncle Jim.

'You wouldn't believe it,' said Uncle Michael. 'It was like...flying.'

My father thought about this. 'So how come you took so long to get down here?'

'I had to do a detour...to get to the motorway.'

This sounded strange, but people would go miles out of their way just to say they'd driven on the M1.

'How fast did you go?' asked Andrew.

'The clock was knocking 90,' said Uncle Michael.

'Why buy a Citroën?' asked Uncle Jim.

'So many reasons,' said Uncle Michael. 'Design, innovation and...engineering. The suspension is revolutionary Watch this.'

He started the engine, and astonishingly the vehicle seemed to rise off the ground, levitate. Then when he switched off it gently lowered itself again. We'd never seen anything like it. I took my father's hand for security.

'Why does it do that then?' said my father.

'Well it's the...it's...it's...'

'It's hydropneumatic self-levelling suspension,' said Andrew. 'All Citroëns have had it since 1954. Instead of the normal spring suspension that British and American cars have, the Citroën rides on gas. Nitrogen isn't it, Uncle Michael?'

'That's... about it,' said Uncle Michael.

'How much was it?' asked Uncle Jim.

'Cheaper than a British car.'

'I notice you've got 32,000 on the clock,' said my father.

'I prefer second-hand cars,' said Uncle Michael. 'They keep their value better.'

Uncle Michael had an answer for every query. The men were stumped. The women cooed. No one could deny the Citroën had style. It wasn't just functional like an Austin, or brash like a Vauxhall. The Citroën said: look at me, I'm a work of art; this is how beautiful cars can be.

Uncle Michael offered his packet of Player's round. All the men begrudgingly took one.

'Tell you something else,' said Uncle Michael, and winked, 'the girls love a Citroën.'

And this was really why the others were a bit suspicious of Uncle Michael. He was a ladies' man.

The thing was, in those days you just didn't buy foreign cars. We all believed that British cars were the best – they sold worldwide after all. Anyone in town who had bought foreign was remarked on with disdain, as if their cars defined them. One man who drove a Fiat was also a member of the lifeboat crew, and if he were to save you from drowning you'd say you were rescued by 'that bloke who drives the Fiat'.

Foreign cars weren't trusted. They were thought to be lightweight and enigmatic: characteristics that summed up Uncle Michael perfectly.

On Sunday we quickly cleaned our Hillman then went along with our buckets and sponges and offered to wash the Citroën. Uncle Michael laughed. 'I've never washed it.'

'How do you keep it clean?'

'I take it through the car wash.'

A car wash?! Our uncle had been through a car wash?! Was there no end to his louche lifestyle? First the motorway and now this. I couldn't wait to tell them at school.

'Where do you go to get a car wash?' said Andrew.

'Birmingham.'

We washed the Citroën and he took us to town to buy an ice cream. He parked on the seafront, and as the engine stopped and the hydraulic suspension lowered the frame, people gathered round. Uncle Michael tapped another Player's on its packet, then stood leaning against the car, wreathed in smoke. He might as well have been Marlon Brando. People asked him questions and he answered them all happily, unless they were to do with anything technical, which Andrew fielded.

'What does DS mean?' said one chap.

'DS means *déesse*,' said Uncle Michael. 'Which means goddess in French. It's the Brigitte Bardot of motors.' He repeated his line, and the little crowd laughed.

Whenever we went on a family outing, all the women wanted to go in the Citroën. That left the men and boys all squashed into the Hillman.

We watched Uncle Michael up ahead driving with his elbow sticking out of the window, flicking ash into the slipstream.

'That Michael needs to meet a good woman,' said Uncle Jim.

The last thing Uncle Michael needed was a good woman. He'd stop driving wonderful cars and get a Hillman.

'He'll probably find a divorcée,' said Uncle Harvey. 'He said he likes second-hand.'

We drove to Corfe Castle. The Citroën caused as much of a stir among the visitors as the Norman castle keep did. One man asked us if he could take a picture.

'General de Gaulle drives one of these, you know,' said Uncle Michael as he held the door open for Grandma.

'Really?' said Grandma and preened herself in the vanity mirror. She was in a car driven by heads of state – French ones, but so what?

The trouble with cars in those days, no matter what country they came from, was simply that they broke down a lot. A man with his head under a steaming bonnet by the side of the road was a common sight. On the plus side, cars were often easy enough to repair yourself, or at least patch up until you got to a garage. If the fan belt broke you made repairs with a necktie or, better still, a woman's stocking. If the engine wasn't firing you could take a wire brush to the plugs.

But when, on the way home that afternoon, the steering on Uncle Michael's Citroën grew heavy, the gears stopped working and the suspension lowered the car gracefully but emphatically to the ground, no one had a clue what to do.

The men lifted the bonnet and reacted as if it was their first sight of an alien species. 'Never seen one like that before,' said Uncle Harvey, who had appointed himself chief mechanic.

'What are those green things?' asked my father.

'Those are the... the... I don't know what they are,' said

Uncle Michael, who could well have been looking under the bonnet for the first time himself.

'Have you got a handbook?' said Uncle Harvey.

Uncle Michael dug out the handbook.

'This is French,' said Uncle Harvey.

'Yes, I thought that was strange myself,' said Uncle Michael.

My mother could speak French and she translated as best she could. 'If the stop sign comes on, stop,' she read.

'What does it say about hydraulic failure?' said Uncle Harvey.

'It says "stains on the fabric can be easily cleaned with warm soapy water".'

'When did you last have it serviced?' asked my father.

Uncle Michael shrugged. 'It was... it must have been... Actually, I've never had it serviced.'

'Who did you buy it off?'

'Just some bloke.'

All the men shook their heads and sucked in sharply.

A car was waved down. The driver peered under the bonnet. 'Foreign cars,' he said, shaking his head.

He gave my father a lift to the nearest phone box. Mr Goodall was called out and he soon arrived with a tow truck.

'Well well,' he said, as he peered under the bonnet.

'What do you think it is?' asked Uncle Michael.

'I reckon it's the, er... what are those green things there?'

'No one knows,' said Uncle Harvey.

He towed the Citroën back to base. My father made two trips in the Hillman and ferried us all back home. By the time we got in it was almost dark. 'We've missed *Bonanza*,' said Grandma.

Mr Goodall said he was pretty sure it was the alternator. But it was nothing to do with the alternator. Neither Mr Goodall nor anyone else in town knew what it was. The Citroën stood in his workshop, its flat face now making it look gloomy rather than stylish. Uncle Michael had to walk into town to buy his cigarettes.

At the end of their visit Aunts Edith, Ethel and Gwen, and Uncles Jim and Harvey went home on the train. Uncle Michael sat and watched TV and waited for news. Eventually a Citroën mechanic from Bournemouth came over and diagnosed a hydropneumatic breakdown. It needed a new part that would take three weeks to arrive.

'Why so long?' asked Uncle Michael.

'It's a Bank holiday,' said the mechanic. 'Also, it's got to come from France.'

My father took Uncle Michael to the station in the Hillman. He would take the train home and come down again to pick the car up. 'This isn't a bad little car, is it?' he said, looking round the Hillman.

'Not bad,' said my father. 'It gets from A to B.'

That was my father's favourite phrase. I imagined it on his gravestone: 'He got from A to B.'

Uncle Michael sold the Citroën over the winter. Next time he came down he had a Vauxhall Victor.

He also had a fiancée.

Chapter 4

Patrolman Nesbitt

When I was eight years old I joined the Cub Scouts. Every Tuesday evening the pack met at the Methodist Church Hall and played British bulldog, sang and tied knots. In the summer we went out onto the Downs and baked apples.

Once a year came 'Bob-a-Job' week. This was basically child labour. You knocked on the door of a house and said 'Bob-a-Job' and the residents could then make you paint the entire downstairs, landscape the garden or rewire the house, and all for a shilling.

The one job that was fair was car washing, and if ever anyone said, 'I've nothing for you to do,' we always suggested: 'Wash your car, sir?'

All we boys were well practised at car washing. It was how we earned our board and lodging at home. It was an hour's work to do a proper job: a wash and a chamois leather finish and, if the owner had a tin of Simoniz, a good shine.

My father was always interested to hear whose house we'd been to and what sort of car they had.

'We did Mr Price's. He's got a Morris Traveller.'

'Strange, I would have put him down as a Ford sort of man. Easy car to clean?'

He always asked this as well – whether a particular car was easy to clean – which sounded odd, but each car was different: some had more chrome than others, some needed stepladders to get to the roof. The Morris Traveller had a wooden frame and should probably have been treated with creosote.

'A Morris is fairly easy,' I said. 'Harder than a Mini, but easier than a Rover.'

He nodded. I wondered if later he went to his desk and made a note in his logbook.

One day I came home and told him I'd washed the Hendrys' car. 'It was a Vauxhall Cresta,' I said, before he could ask.

He nodded in approval. The Hendrys were a Vauxhall Cresta sort of family. 'Easy car to clean?'

'Not really. Too many badges. Fiddly.'

'What sort of badges?'

'One was an RAC badge.'

'RAC?! Are you sure?'

'Positive.'

He fell silent. The news that the Hendrys were members of the RAC had made his pipe hang from the corner of his mouth. When we sat down to eat that evening he was so quiet my mother asked him if anything was wrong.

'No, nothing's wrong. On the contrary, today is an important day. I've made a decision.'

We stopped eating. Was it good news or bad?

'I've decided it's time we joined a motoring organization.'

Unlike today when your choice of motoring organization depends entirely on who gives you the cheapest breakdown insurance, in 1960 the decision was life-changing. Being a member of the AA or the RAC said as much about you as your religion.

'You're an RAC man,' said my mother. 'You smoke a pipe, you wear a blazer; you were in the RAF. Also the blue RAC badge goes a lot better with the Hillman's colour scheme. The gold of the AA would clash.'

Andrew differed, but that was because, as usual, he had done the research. 'The AA have got more emergency boxes than the RAC, plus the AA is the motoring organization of the modern motorist. The RAC is for squares.'

'You mean, the AA is... "with it"?' said my father.

'Yes.'

'Mmm.'

He cringed. How awful it would be to be 'with it'.

He did what he always did in situations like this and wrote off for literature. The AA and RAC details were very similar. Historically there was little in it. Both organizations were founded around the turn of the century as motoring lobbyists, campaigning against police-imposed speed limits. Now they were defined by their roadside assistance for members, and their brightly painted emergency kiosks.

Most importantly though, both organizations were represented by patrolmen, knights of the road who wore military jackets, riding boots and jodhpurs as they roamed the highways on motorbikes – tool-kit in a side-car – looking for drivers in distress. Best of all, whenever they passed a member, they saluted.

Mother was right: my father was by inclination an RAC man. But, as ever, he was aware of his place. To him RAC members were the elite. AA members were the middle classes, the Sunday afternoon outing brigade, and that was where, if he was honest, he felt happiest. This dilemma was brilliantly captured a couple of years later in a TV *Comedy Playhouse* by Tony Hancock's writers, Galton and Simpson. A Bentley driven by an RAC member comes nose to nose on a country lane with a banger bearing an AA badge. The road is blocked; one car will have to give way. The RAC owner pulls rank, but the AA owner stands his ground. An AA patrolman turns up and tries to persuade the RAC member to back up, but then an RAC patrolman arrives and picks on the AA member. Even at my age the class politics were clear. My father watched it between the gaps in his fingers.

'Mr Cassell the fishmonger is a member of the AA,' I told him, having just cleaned his car for 'Bob-a-Job' week.

'That fits,' said my father.

'But Mr Nation is a member of the RAC.'

My father stroked his chin.

'What does Mr Nation do?' I asked.

'He works for the Inland Revenue.'

The odds were leaning in favour of the AA. Then my mother came in and announced: 'I've just read in the paper that the RAC have women patrolmen, or rather patrolwomen.'

And that clinched it.

As soon as our AA membership arrived my father secured the badge proudly to the radiator grill on the Hillman and took us out for a drive, looking for a patrolman to salute us.

First we went to fill up at Mr Goodall's. 'The Esso sign means happy motoring, the Esso sign means happy motoring, the Esso...'

'Yes, yes, all right,' said my father.

Mr Goodall had taken to singing the new TV advert as he filled your tank. 'Can't help it Mr Wallington. It's so catchy. I reckon they've come up with a winner. Almost as good as "Bom bom bom bom, Esso Blue".'

'Are you RAC or AA?' asked Andrew.

'Me?' said Mr Goodall. 'I'm both.'

Both! You couldn't be both. It was like supporting Arsenal *and* Spurs.

'I'm a businessman. I have to be impartial,' said Mr Goodall. 'Got to keep my customers happy,' and he handed us a roll of stamps.

'What's this?' asked my father.

'Green Shield Stamps.'

'I don't want them.'

'You collect them and then you exchange them for free gifts.' He gave us a catalogue. 'Look, you get a carriage clock, or a milk jug...'

'I don't want them.'

'Or a leather map holder.'

A leather map holder. My father's eyes lit up. He took the catalogue. 'Don't tell your mother about this, all right?'

We set off looking for an AA man. 'There's one,' said my father, and pointed up ahead.

He was right. Four cars ahead of us was the distinctive yellow and black motorbike and side-car, with a khaki-clad patrolman astride it.

My father overtook all the cars in front, then overtook the patrolman. But he didn't salute us. In fact he might

even have scowled at us for getting too close. We yelled
and waved, but he ignored us.

'He couldn't see the badge, could he?' said my father.
'He has to be coming from the opposite direction.'

We stopped and turned round, but we couldn't find
him again. As we drove home an RAC patrolman passed
and ignored us.

The first salute we got was one Sunday when we set off to
have a picnic in the New Forest and then to visit Aunt
Monica to show off our new sister. My mother sat in the
front seat with the baby on her lap. We sat in the back, eyes
peeled for patrolmen.

'We need petrol,' said my mother.

'No we don't,' said my father.

Despite our attempts at secrecy my mother had quickly
discovered the Green Shield Stamps catalogue and had just
as quickly become addicted. She would have been happy
to drive round and empty the tank just to fill it up again
and get more stamps. The moment she saw the range of
gifts she became starry-eyed and immediately made a list.
At the top were the cut glass wine goblets. The leather
map holder dropped way, way down.

We set off east into Hampshire. Aunt Monica was no
blood relation, but for some reason had been awarded the
title. Andrew and I didn't like visiting her simply because
she had no children of her own and her house felt like a
museum. You couldn't move without knocking over
porcelain. 'Why does Aunt Monica never come to visit
us?' I said.

'She can't drive,' said my father.

I imagined this poor woman who never left the house because she couldn't drive. 'How did people travel before cars?' I asked.

'Ssh, your father's driving.'

But then a few miles on my mother said, 'I can't drive either.'

'No,' said my father. Matter settled.

'I think I'll learn to drive.'

My father laughed.

'What's funny?'

'Nothing's funny. There's just no need for you to learn to drive.'

'Why not?'

'Because I drive.'

'I might want to go out in the car without you.'

'Why would you want to do that?'

'Something might happen to you,' interjected Andrew. 'And then Mum would become like Aunt Monica.'

The idea of our mother turning into Aunt Monica was appalling. All that brown furniture.

'Stop here!' yelled my mother.

Our family had embraced the Sunday outing like no other family I knew. We each had our role. My father of course was the driver. The children's role was to sit still and quiet and not distract the driver, even though the driver was blowing pipe smoke in their faces for the whole journey. My mother's role was to spot good picnic sites. This was why she was prone to yelling out, 'Stop here!'

On the odd occasion, my father was able to stop where she wanted him to, and we'd have lunch in a meadow with a stream running by, shaded by willows.

Just as often though, my father would yell back, 'I can't stop here, I've got a coach behind me.'

'Well pull over.'

'I can't just pull over.'

'We've missed it now. Do a U turn.'

'I can't just do a U turn.'

'Well pull into this gateway.'

'I can't just pull into a gateway.'

This would go on for miles. My father would lose his temper and we'd end up sitting in a lay-by eating crisps. Which is what happened on this particular Sunday. My mother's mood darkened. She returned to the learning-to-drive debate because she knew it annoyed him.

'Learning to drive would be good for my independence.'

'Independence is overrated.'

'There are lots of things I'd like to do on my own.'

'Like what?'

'None of your business.'

I leaned my head against the window to watch the traffic go by, and then there he was, a man in khaki on a yellow and black motorbike, just dropping his hand from a salute. An AA man.

'I saw one! I saw one!'

'There are ponies everywhere,' said my father. 'No need to shout.'

'I saw an AA man. And he saluted.'

'No you didn't.'

'Yes I did. I saw him.'

'I didn't see him,' said Andrew.

'Nor me,' said my father.

'You were arguing,' I said.

'I think I would have seen an AA man saluting, don't you?'

'I saw him.'

'And we weren't arguing,' said my mother. 'We were discussing.'

'I saw him. I did.'

'I'm going to have driving lessons,' said my mother. 'I've decided.'

AA members had many perks. Besides a handbook there was a gazetteer giving information on hotels and garages and when it was half-day closing in Lichfield. Members could have personalized route planners made to order, plus they were given the priceless AA key, which would open the yellow and black kiosks that stood like sentry boxes at lonely roadside spots.

'What do they have inside?' I asked.

'All sorts of things,' said my father, clearly not knowing.

'Can we have a look inside one?'

'Only if we break down.'

How I longed to break down so we could call an AA man out. But of course as soon as we joined the AA the Hillman entered a sustained period of good health.

'Can't we just have a look in one?' I asked.

'AA boxes are there for an emergency; they're not playthings.'

Six months went by. We didn't break down. It just wasn't fair. Kelvin Peak at school broke down and he said in the RAC box there were sandwiches and pop and crisps. As well as a bright blue telephone that you didn't have to dial.

'What's in the AA box?' he asked me.

'Not sure.'

'RAC boxes are much better.'

'No they're not.'

'How do you know?'

Another boy at school, Dennis, had a father who was in the AA. 'Has your car ever broken down?' I asked.

'Lots of times.'

'Tell me what's in the AA box?'

'We're not members of the AA.'

'But your car has a badge.'

'My dad bought it second-hand. It was already on there.'

'Do the patrolmen salute you?'

'Yes. It's great.'

I told my father when I got home. 'That's not fair, is it?'

'Life's not fair, son,' he said, and tapped his pipe on the sole of his shoe.

The Hillman motored for a year without breaking down. 'Joining the AA was a waste of money,' said my mother.

'The reason we haven't broken down,' said Andrew, 'is that we're members of the AA.'

I couldn't grasp the logic there, but I didn't feel able to argue with it either.

Then one day we were on another of our outings, this time with Grandma, going to see her friends who had retired down to Devon. She was crowbarred in between my brother and me on the back seat. My knees were jammed together, my shoulder pressed into the door; Grandma sat clutching her handbag like the reins on a horse. She smelt of scones and talcum powder.

We got lost. 'You should have gone straight on at the last junction,' said my mother, who was map reading with an unrestrained one-year-old on her lap.

'I did go straight on.'

'No, you forked left.'

He stopped the car and had a look at the map.

'We should have turned right miles back,' said my father.

'No we shouldn't. We turn right at the junction with the A354.'

'No we don't.'

'Who's navigating?'

'You are and you're lost.'

'Don't row in front the children,' said Grandma.

'They're not rowing, they're discussing,' said Andrew.

It was a scenario being played out in many cars all over the country on a Sunday afternoon 50 years before satnavs.

They drove on a little further, hoping for a road sign.

'Stop now!' yelled my mother.

My father slammed on the brakes. Grandma's hand went instinctively to her hat. Her elbow hit me in the temple.

'Are we having a picnic?' I asked.

'We passed an AA box,' said my mother.

'So?' said my father.

'You've got your key, haven't you? You could phone up for directions.'

'You can't do that.'

'Why not?'

'It's not allowed. It's only for breakdowns.'

'Oh for heaven's sake!'

My father was torn. They were lost and he knew it. But

for a man to admit he was lost, particularly to a motoring organization, well, they'd probably laugh at him. Word would get round the patrolmen; the story would be told at the Christmas party. If my father ever did have to call out a patrolman he'd say, 'Oh yes, Mr Wallington, the chap who got lost on the A35.'

But my father couldn't waste time. We were due to arrive in Devon in time for Grandma to use the toilet. If that didn't happen, the situation would quickly become unpleasant. He said to my mother, 'You go and phone, say you're the driver.'

'Why me?'

'Because... I need to stay with the car. We're on a busy main road. Anything could happen.'

My mother knew exactly what was happening of course. She said, 'I can't say I'm a driver.'

'Why not?'

'Because I can't drive. Remember?'

'They won't know that.'

'I wouldn't know what to say. Not being a driver.'

He gritted his teeth. 'All right. Maybe you *should* have lessons.'

My mother took the key and marched up to the box still clutching the baby. Andrew ran after her.

'Come back!' yelled my father.

But he was too late; I was out there as well, following them to the box. My mother turned the key and we all peered inside.

No sandwiches, no tea in a flask. Just a fire extinguisher, some maps, an oil lamp, a waste paper bin and, on the wall, a bright yellow phone.

My mother picked up the phone. She didn't know what

to do without a dial. She started as a voice came out of the mouthpiece. 'Hello. What box are you at?'

'What's the box number?' my mother whispered.

'It's there on the wall,' said Andrew.

Baby Jane started to cry. My mother handed the phone to Andrew.

'Hello. We're lost,' he said. Then he gave the box number, said, 'Thank you very much,' and put the phone down. 'Patrolman Nesbitt is on his way.'

When we told my father his head hit the steering wheel in shame. He might even have driven off, but within a minute a motorbike and side-car had pulled up.

Patrolman Nesbitt was an unlikely saviour. He was short and tubby with a toothbrush moustache, but he did have a cape on, and goggles which gave him a certain Batman quality.

He politely pointed out the correct route to my father, who said things like: 'Yes, I thought that was the case, the wife was navigating.'

Then, without asking, Patrolman Nesbitt lifted the Hillman's bonnet and began to check the fluid levels. He called out, 'Could use a little oil sometime soon, sir.'

'Can you tell us where the nearest public convenience is?' shouted Grandma from the back seat.

Patrolman Nesbitt marked it on the map, then saluted us, and wished us a pleasant trip. I hoped he might rev his bike up and roar off, but he didn't; he went into the AA box and closed the door behind him.

'He's going to read the paper, I expect,' said Grandma.

My father quietly fumed for the rest of the journey. No one had ever dared question his oil level before. He never came nearer to cancelling his membership.

The rest of us were very happy with this first brush with the AA. My mother was going to have driving lessons. My grandma got to empty her bladder in time. And I, at only age eight, had decided on a career path: I was going to be an AA patrolman.

Chapter 5

His and Hers

My father may have been uneasy at the idea of my mother learning to drive, but British motor manufacturers were all in favour. Having sold a car to just about every man in the country, by the start of the sixties they were turning their attention to women. The major marques all had models which didn't say as much but were clearly marketed at women drivers: the Riley Elf, the Hillman Imp, the Morris Mini Minor. The manufacturers had made us a nation of car owners and now they wanted to make us a nation of two-car families. They had my mother in their sights.

My father wasn't going to be a pushover though.

'I'm not sure about Mr Norbert,' he said. 'His shoes weren't very clean.'

'What have his shoes got to do with it?' said my mother.

'Never trust a man without clean shoes or collar.'

Mr Norbert was the third driving instructor to be interviewed.

'Mr Duchamp had clean shoes,' said my mother.

'Yes, but he was French.'

'What have you got against the French?'

'In this case only one thing: they drive on the other side of the road.'

It wasn't that my father was against the idea of my mother driving – he'd come to terms with that; he'd discovered that the Minister for Overseas Development had a female chauffeur, and for some reason that made things easier. What he was really frightened of was losing proprietary rights over the car. Despite my mother's early attempts to turn the car into a mobile extension of the sitting room, the car was my father's space. The door pockets had tobacco in them. The boot contained his wellingtons and the *For Sale* placards that he attached to properties. He didn't want my mother taking over, tidying up, replacing his stuff with hers. To most men at that time their cars were like sheds. Women were allowed in them but couldn't fuss. My father wanted it to smell of pipe cleaners and mud, not perfume. 'I bet you the first thing she does,' he confided in us boys, 'is move the seat forward.'

'Can't you move it back?' said Andrew.

'Yes, but that's not the point.'

He said to my mother, 'Just say you do pass your test – and it's not as easy as it looks – what are you going to drive?'

'I thought I'd drive the car.'

'I need it for work.'

'At the weekends, or the evenings. Or the days you don't need it for work.'

'I need it for work every day. And some evenings. And most weekends.'

'In that case, we'll have to buy another car.'

He swallowed smoke and started a coughing fit.

This was precisely the sort of argument the manufacturers wanted my parents to have, of course. It was surprising they didn't use a similar scene in a TV advert. 'I need the car for work.'

'But I need the car for when I discover we're out of washing powder and you won't have a clean shirt for the morning.'

'There's only one thing for it then, my dear: we must buy another car.'

My mother tried to underline the advantages. 'I can take the children to the beach. You won't have to take Grandma to the library any more.'

And she was always trying to impress him with little facts about women drivers. 'Look, it says here women are better drivers than men.'

'I find that hard to believe.'

'The insurance companies say as much.'

'How do they know?'

'They know because women have fewer accidents.'

'That's because there are fewer women drivers.'

'That's because men don't encourage women to drive.'

My father smiled and nodded the way he always did when he was about to say something condescending. 'You see, what you've got to realize is driving isn't simply about not having accidents.'

It was hard to argue with an opinion like that. But she wasn't going to be dissuaded. She said, 'I'm not discussing this any more. I'm going to have my first lesson this weekend.'

'Very well,' said my father. 'Saturday morning. We'll start with hand signals.'

'We?'

'Yes.'

'You're going to teach me?'

'Well we're not wasting money on an instructor.'

The hand signals lesson took place at the kitchen table.

They turned the chairs round and sat next to each other. My mother held a large saucepan lid as the wheel.

'Traffic lights ahead,' said my father, and my mother put her arm out and gracefully performed the 'slowing down' wave.

'Turn left in 50 yards!' said my father and she stuck her arm out and did the circular motion.

'Now, I want you to change gear and signal turning right.'

There was a loud clatter as my mother dropped the saucepan lid.

After a month of learning to drive in the kitchen she insisted he let her try in the car.

'There you go,' he said, 'trying to run before you can walk.'

He was more nervous than she was. I think he would have liked one of us boys to walk in front of the Hillman with a red flag, but my mother took us round to Grandma's. We sat down in front of the TV with a drink and a piece of malt loaf to watch *Whirlybirds*. Within 15 minutes my father was back to collect us.

'Where's mum?'

'She's, er... she's... gone for a little walk.'

She came back after dark and the search for a driving instructor started.

Nine years old and I was going through a period of obsession with emergency vehicles. I was constantly running round the school playground making siren noises: 'ding, ding, ding, ding' for a British vehicle; 'na na na na na na' for an American one.

There were reasons for this. One was watching too much television; another was our school's proximity to the town fire station. One afternoon as we were filing out, an engine came swinging out of the red doors opposite and sped off, bell clanging, firemen clinging to the back. Nothing strange about that, until I got home and found them parked outside my house. The living room was full of soot and in front of the hearth where the dog normally lay was an overweight fireman. He was on his hands and knees trying to peer up the chimney.

'All taken care of,' he said to my mother, and as he stood up his medals fell off.

'Think I'll have that cup of tea now.'

It was just a chimney fire and easily dealt with. Half the crew hadn't even bothered to get off the truck. They sat on top smoking, which seemed ironic even to a nine-year-old.

I stood on the pavement looking up at the huge red engine.

'Want to have a look inside?'

'Yes please.'

They hoisted me up. It was all hoses and helmets. I sat in the driver's seat; my hands could hardly reach the wheel.

'Can we have the siren on?'

'No.'

It didn't matter. Five minutes at the wheel of the big red beast and I went seamlessly from wanting to be an AA man when I grew up, to wanting to be a fireman.

This career change didn't last long. One day shortly afterwards the bus didn't come to take us home from school. We started to walk, but somehow, despite living in the same town all our lives, we got lost. When we didn't show up at home my mother did the only thing she could do and called the police. We were walking along the seafront when a police car pulled up and a WPC got out.

We were told to get into the back. We sat there guilty as charged. A radio crackled. The WPC turned round and offered us a wine gum.

'Can we have the siren on?' I asked.

'No.'

My mother was fraught and tearful. But the police still sat down for a cup of tea.

When my father came home she said, 'This is why we should have two cars.'

He knew when to say nothing. He took us out into the driveway to play cricket.

'I've changed my mind again,' I said. 'I want to be a policeman when I grow up.'

'Good for you,' he said.

With fire engine and police car ticked off, I had only an ambulance to go for the full set of emergency vehicle rides, which, I was sure, would be a playground coup. An ambulance was going to be tricky though. To get a ride in one of those you needed to be on your way to hospital.

'You could jump off the garage roof,' said Andrew, being unusually helpful. 'Or you could stick something metal into the electric socket. That would probably do it.'

I climbed on the garage roof to do a recce. I balanced on the edge, closed my eyes and imagined jumping off. A voice said, 'I'm looking for Mrs Wallington.'

I opened one eye to see a white Austin 1100 parked in the road with a big, red letter L on a plinth secured to the roof, and in the driveway a bald man in a blazer with a row of pens clipped to his top pocket in order of height, right to left.

'That's not an ambulance is it?' I asked.

'No. It's a driving school car.'

'Does it have a siren?'

'Is your mother in?'

He was Mr Pardew from East Dorset Motoring School. I climbed down and took him inside to be interviewed.

My father looked him over. He had passed the handshake test easily enough, and the lack of facial hair was in his favour. He was promising.

'Smoke a pipe?' asked my father.

'Don't smoke sir,' said Mr Pardew.

My mother sensed he was going to be rejected on the grounds that you couldn't trust a man who didn't smoke, so she intervened and asked if she could have a trial lesson. 'Certainly, Mrs Wallington,' said Mr Pardew, and produced his driving licence and Ministry of Transport Approved Driving Instructor certificate for anyone who wanted to inspect them. No one did. So he led my mother out to his car and held the driver's door open for her.

My father was astonished that Mr Pardew was going to let her just drive away from the house without having any idea whether she could operate a vehicle or not, without even any time at the kitchen table. He took Mr Pardew to one side and said, 'Listen, I've taught her the basics: hand signals, how to work the clutch, mirror use, that sort of thing, but she's... you know.'

'Leave it with me sir.'

We all stood and watched my mother happily drive away with a strange man. 'Are you going to follow them?' said Andrew.

My father had a think about that, but then said, 'No, there's a boxing match on TV. Come on.'

But he didn't really watch it. He kept looking at the clock. As the hour mark approached he was out in the road watching for the little Austin to return.

It came smoothly down the hill with my mother still at the wheel. My father gave the vehicle a quick inspection: it didn't look damaged; neither did my mother; nor Mr Pardew.

She got out and thanked Mr Pardew and said, 'Same time next week?'

'Certainly, Mrs Wallington.'

My father waited on the kerb, expecting a report from at least one of them, but Mr Pardew said, 'Good afternoon,' and drove away, while my mother went straight into the house.

She never talked to my father about the lessons. When he asked her what Mr Pardew had taught her she said, 'He told me that the driving test was introduced in 1935.'

'And?'

'And he said something very interesting. Did you know that during the Suez Crisis there were no driving tests? Driving instructors were employed to implement rationing.'

So he took to quizzing Mr Pardew at the end of the lesson before he could drive off. 'So, how's my wife coming along?'

'Oh, Mrs Wallington is doing very well. I think she'll be ready for her test soon.'

'Her test! Already? Is that wise?'

'Next month perhaps.'

For the first time it dawned on my father that this was serious.

Mr Besant from next door had seen the driving school car. 'She's learning to drive, I see?'

'That's right,' said my father and rolled his eyes.

Mr Besant said, 'Elaine had the same idea,' and he rolled his eyes as well. But this was because Elaine had struggled. 'She can't pass the test,' he said. 'She's taken it six times.'

Now they both rolled their eyes.

My father clutched at this news. Just because my mother was taking her test didn't mean she'd pass. It might take her years. When she came back from her next lesson, and said that Mr Pardew had booked her in for a test in three weeks, he said, 'Good, but don't get too excited.'

'Why not?'

'No one passes their test the first time.'

'Mr Pardew says lots of his clients do.'

'Learning to drive and passing your test are two different things.'

'He says the people who don't pass the first time are mostly men.'

The day came. Mr Pardew called early in the morning before we all went to school. 'Well, good luck,' said my father. 'And even if do you fail, I want you to know I'm very proud of you.'

'I'm not going to fail,' she said.

'What I mean is, you've made your point. You don't want to be one of these people who takes it six times.'

'I think she'll be fine,' said Mr Pardew.

And of course she was fine. When we came out of school the Hillman was there to pick us up, but behind the wheel was my mother rather than my father. She drove us home smoothly and with a straight back and didn't smoke a pipe.

We sat in the back seat in silence.

'Aren't you going to say well done?' she said.

'Well done,' I mumbled.

'If you've got the car, how's Dad going to get home?' said Andrew.

'Oh, I'll go and pick him up later or he'll walk. I've got to take Grandma to the library.'

On the back seat there were two new cushions.

The class was playing relay races in the playground. It was a damp autumn morning and the ground was littered with wet leaves. We were wearing gym shoes, and I slipped and took what felt like a perfectly normal tumble. But then I couldn't get up; my leg wouldn't move. I could tell something serious had happened by the way class was cancelled and I was surrounded by teachers. I was told to lie still. A blanket was put over me. Then across the playground came two men in uniform carrying a stretcher. Ambulance men. Any pain I felt was immediately numbed by the impending thrill.

I was carried down to the ambulance and the stretcher was slid inside. 'Do you want the siren on?' said the driver.

'Yes please!'

He reached up for the switch. The bell started and I knew they'd be able to hear it back in the classroom. I had a broken leg and couldn't remember feeling so happy. I said to the driver, 'If you call in at my house my mother will give you cup of tea.' But he went straight to the hospital in Poole. I imagined you couldn't put the siren on and then stop for tea.

No one came to visit me until the evening. My father had been out all day with clients and for my mother to get to the hospital it would have meant two buses and a ride on a chain ferry.

When they came to see me, the first thing my mother said was: 'We've decided to buy another car.'

It was a green Mini, a car that ducked and dived its way around town, always in a hurry.

Mr Besant saw my mother whizz off in it. He said to my father, 'She passed?'

'Yes, of course.'

'First time?'

'First time,' he said proudly.

The purchase of the second car had, despite the expense, been the simple answer to my father's concerns, and now he looked pleased with his wife's success, coupled with the fact that he didn't have to take Grandma to the bloody library any more.

Mr Besant was a bit put out. 'First time? Who was your instructor?'

'Pardew. East Dorset Motoring School. Decent chap.'

Chapter 6

Dinky Days

Every Saturday my friend Dennis would come round. 'Shall we play Dinky toys?' he said.

Well of course we were going to play Dinky toys. We always played Dinky toys. What else were we going to play?

We both had a boxful: the usual saloon cars, but also specialist sub-collections. I collected anything with a siren on top. Dennis, by contrast, was into commercial vehicles. He had a petrol tanker, a bread van, a flat-bed truck and his favourite, a BBC Television Outside Broadcast Mobile Control Room, complete with cameraman perched on top.

All our imagination and energy was channelled into those model vehicles, and we put them through hell. We played with them indoors, creating a cardboard motorway for them to run on, and we played with them outdoors on the driveway and in the flower beds. 'I wonder if they float?' I said, so we put them in the bath to simulate a car-ferry disaster.

'I wonder if they fly?' said Dennis, rather hopefully in my opinion, but we launched them from the bedroom window anyway.

New neighbours moved in with a nine-year-old son called Philip. We were told to invite him round to play.

'Want to play Dinky toys?' said Dennis.

'Yes please,' said Philip.

We poured our cars onto the floor. Philip said, 'That's not a Dinky toy.'

'Yes it is.'

'It's got windows. It's a Corgi.'

Corgi was Dinky's rival. They marketed themselves with the slogan 'The Ones with Windows'. Dinky responded with rear-wheel suspension; Corgi fought back with bonnets that lifted to display a detailed engine; Dinky countered with boots that opened to reveal luggage. The only people to benefit from this competition were nine-year-old boys. And we didn't care who made what. Until Philip came along we called them all Dinky toys anyway.

Philip knew his Dinky toys better than any child we had ever met. And not just British models.

'I've got a Studebaker Goldenhawk,' he said one day.

Dennis and I hadn't a clue.

'It's from Corgi's American range.'

We didn't believe him. 'Show us it then.'

'It's at home.'

But we never went to Philip's home. He always came to us and he never brought his Dinky toys with him.

The toy shop was just down the hill from school. I went in one day and asked for a Corgi catalogue. There, at the back, was the American list: Buicks, Pontiacs, Cadillacs, and the Studebaker Goldenhawk. But there was one car that stood out above them all: the Chevrolet Impala. It was all fins and fenders and had a grill like a mouthful of perfect teeth. There was even a police car version. The very idea made me run all the way home and put it straight to the top of my Christmas list.

'I've got a new car on my Christmas list too,' said my father.

'A new car! What sort of new car?' we all shouted.

He puffed on his pipe and looked out of the French windows, enjoying being the centre of attention, 'Why is that Dinky toy on top of the garage roof?'

'It flew up there,' I said. 'What sort of car?'

'Not sure yet, have to do the research.'

Normally the announcement of a new car kept me awake at night with anticipation. On this occasion, though, the excitement was mixed with anxiety. I was heavily immersed in playground politics, and the car your family owned was of utmost significance. Dennis's father drove a Wolseley that was so old and beat up that Dennis always asked to be dropped off a good distance from the school gates to avoid humiliation. We just about got away with the Hillman, but a new car could change everything. It could make or break my bid to join the Tree Gang, a group of underachievers so called because they met under the sycamore tree at the far end of the playground. If they'd had any imagination they might have called themselves the Sycamore Gang. But they didn't have. So Tree Gang it was.

I lay awake wondering what my father was going to buy. A Chevrolet Impala would have done the trick, but that wasn't going to happen. I was worried because of late we'd be driving round town and he'd see some desperately boring car like a Rover and say, 'That's a nice car.' I'd say a silent prayer and try to divert him.

'That's a nice car,' I'd say as we passed one of the new Zephyr Zodiacs.

His lip curled. He was more likely to get a tattoo than a Zephyr Zodiac.

I feared the worst. If we got a Rover I'd have no choice but to change school. The Rover 80 actually looked like an old man. It was the only car on the market with jowls.

Then my brother came to the rescue. He asked if, for his birthday treat, we could go to the Motor Show.

'Wonderful idea,' said my father. 'A boys' outing.'

Surely, surrounded by the best that motoring design and technology could offer, he'd be seduced by something a little less like a dinosaur.

In the sixties, the Motor Show was an event right up there with the Trooping of the Colour and the Cup Final. It was the highlight of the manufacturers' calendar, and where they launched their new models. It was glitzy and fashionable, a proud display of the cutting edge of motor technology. It was also the best place to see scantily clad women spread over cars, as my brother confessed to me later.

Earls Court was ablaze with flashing, polished steel. Everywhere you looked were spotless vehicles, straight from the factory, some going round and round on carousels, some poised at dynamic angles, almost all of them with a long-haired girl sitting on the bonnet running her finger down the paintwork, or showing her legs off as she lay on the back seat. The only place you didn't see one was behind the steering wheel.

'But why's she wearing her swimming costume?' I asked my father.

'It's hot,' was his brilliant reply. 'Let's go and have a look at the new 1100.'

Despite being surrounded by the most exciting cars in the world, my father managed to search out the most ordinary. They'd taken the doors off the new Austin 1100, so you could see right through it, but that didn't make it look any more alluring. A salesman handed us a brochure. 'Why isn't he wearing his swimming costume?' I asked.

We moved on to look at the new Hillman. It was on display with two women in cocktail dresses sitting cross-legged in the back seat.

'Good lord,' said my father breathlessly.

Andrew and I put ourselves between him and the car. Maybe this was why he didn't want to bring my mother. 'Look,' he said. 'Automatic transmission.'

Suddenly a crowd of photographers was moving in on the Bristol stand. Pop sensation Adam Faith was being given a tour of the car. Andrew and I joined the throng but couldn't get near enough to see the man. I only knew it was him because I heard someone say, 'I can't stand Adam Faith.'

We should never have left my father alone. He had wandered over to the Rover and was sitting down next to it, opening our packed lunch. We gazed at the giant car as we ate our Marmite sandwiches. 'You know why I like the Rover?' he said.

'Why?'

'Because you wouldn't find Adam Faith driving one.'

He was right there. The Rover was like a tank. It was the kind of car you went to weddings and funerals in. The only thing that made it unique at the motor show was that there were no women sprawled over the bonnet. A salesman with a tie pin and a handlebar moustache saw my father light up his post-picnic pipe. 'Pipe smoker eh?' he said, and he got his own pipe out and struck a match. That was what the Rover was, a car for pipe smokers.

We were getting desperate now. 'How about buying a Cortina?' said Andrew. 'They've just released a GT model.'

'I don't think we're a GT kind of family,' said my father.

There was another stampede as Adam Faith moved on to the Bentley. We stood back and let the photographers pass, but as the crowd thinned, in the distance across the hall there was something sparkling like ice.

'What's that over there?' I said. It was a car, but it was long and low and looked as sleek as a cat.

My father wasn't bothered. He was reading his Rover literature. 'Do you know there's over a ton of steel in a Rover?'

'I know what it is,' said Andrew. 'It's an E-Type Jag.'

Now my father looked up. Like everyone else he couldn't resist those words.

He followed us as we ran over. The E-Type was brilliant white and with its top removed it looked even nearer to the ground. Its wide mouth and long nose made it look fierce, as if it should have been in a cage. There was a man in a lab coat sitting nearby holding a clipboard. He looked like a scientist and he was there to answer technical questions only. 'Are we allowed to touch?' I asked.

'No,' said my father.

'Yes,' said the technician.

I remember touching it and feeling the cold perfection. Then running my finger along the front wing, on and on, until it sloped gently down to the headlight. Andrew did the same. Then, incredibly, so did my father. We were all under the car's spell.

We went to see other cars, but always found ourselves wandering back past the E-Type. My father spoke to the technician. I watched as he nodded, writing down all the statistics he was given. He walked round it one way, then the other. He asked if he could sit in it and the technician opened the door for him. Even my father look transformed at the wheel of an E-Type. He had his pipe in his mouth but didn't light it, out of respect.

We drove home with the football results coming over the radio. The commotion of London was left behind; the blackness of the A30 stretched away westward. With the red tail-lights tracing through the night ahead and the headlights flashing past us, there was something magical about simply being on the move, driving through the dark, warm and comfortable in the arms of the old Hillman. 'What happens if you just keep on driving?' I said.

'You run out of petrol,' said my father.

'But if you fill up and keep on driving again?'

'You get to the end of the road.'

'And what happens if you take another road?'

'You get to the end of *that* road.'

'Is there a road which is the endest of all ends of roads?'

He thought about this. 'Yes, I suppose there is.'

'Where?'

'You'll know when you get there.'

I fell silent again, and imagined my father had decided to buy an E-Type instead of a Rover, and I saw myself being dropped off at the school gates and everyone in the Tree Gang stopping what they were doing and watching my father, who was wearing a white chunky pullover and a jaunty cap at the wheel. He waved to everyone and then roared off like Stirling Moss. The Tree Gang didn't ask me to join because they all wanted to join my gang, in fact everyone in the school wanted to be in my gang, even the teachers.

Christmas was getting closer. Dennis and Philip came round one Saturday. 'Shall we play Dinky toys?' said Dennis.

I had already emptied my box on the floor and was going 'Brmm brmm' in a series of different pitches denoting gear changes around the room. Dennis quickly joined in. Philip, however, appeared half-hearted. He didn't even make reversing noises when he pushed his cars backwards.

Dennis and I informed each other what we wanted for Christmas. I told him about the Chevrolet Impala police car. He told me about the glazier's van he wanted which even had sheets of glass clasped in a wooden frame to the side of the vehicle.

'What do you want, Philip?'

Philip shrugged. 'To be honest I'm bored with Dinky toys. I think I might get something completely different.' He spoke with such an adult tone it sounded like he was going to ask for a Fair Isle pullover.

Whether my parents had done anything about the Chevrolet police car I didn't know. What I did know was that, as usual, my father was making us a Christmas present, on this occasion a model garage for all our Dinky toys. He wanted this to be a surprise, but it was a poorly kept secret.

Andrew had found it under the bed in the spare room as early as October. It was just a base with a forecourt and buildings drawn out, but it was clear what it was going to be. Each week we'd creep in and see how it was coming along. Pumps appeared, a workshop and an office. Then the fortnight before Christmas the word *Esso* was painted onto a sign and stuck on a pole.

'I bet he puts a wooden Mr Goodall in there somewhere,' said Andrew.

A week before the big day my father said, 'So, what are you hoping for for Christmas?'

'A Chevrolet Impala police car,' I said for the hundredth time.

My father nodded. 'You know what I think you should ask Father Christmas for?'

'What?'

'A garage for you to put all your cars in, and even drive them into, to have them repaired and filled up with petrol.'

If I hadn't already seen the finished product I would have said, 'No, I don't want anything like that.' But even as a self-centred nine-year-old I could see the pain such a tactless comment would have caused, so I said, 'Good idea, I'll put it on the list, just below the CHEVROLET IMPALA POLICE CAR.'

Why was this so difficult? Buying presents for my father was easy. You got him driving gloves. I never actually saw him wear them, but he did his best to feign surprise and look thrilled. In fact everyone in our family was good at feigning surprise and looking thrilled. It was what we excelled at at Christmas.

'Wow! Look, a garage. Fantastic!' I said, desperately

looking to see if there was a Chevrolet Impala hidden somewhere within its recesses. There wasn't. But it all worked out in the end. I collected enough money from my combined aunts to buy my own, and it only took Dennis to say how much he wished he had a garage for all his cars to make me very proud of my father's gift, even if it did start to fall to bits on Boxing Day.

Dennis and I wondered whether Philip would be keen to play with the garage; it might even reignite his interest in Dinky toys. We asked him round, but for the first time he said no, we were to go to his house.

We carried the garage over. Philip stood in the hallway not knowing what to do with us. 'What's that?' he said.

'It's a garage for Dinky toys,' said Dennis.

Philip said nothing.

'Where are your Dinky toys?' I said.

'In their boxes,' said Philip.

'Well get them out,' said Dennis.

Philip took us up to his bedroom. On a shelf above his bed was a stack of Dinky car boxes. He took one down, and slid the car out carefully onto the carpet. It didn't have a mark on it. Nor did the box. He unpacked the others and lined them up carefully. They looked as pristine as the cars at the Motor Show.

'Have you ever played with them in the garden?' said Dennis.

Philip shook his head.

'You never throw them out of the window?' I said.

Philip looked at me oddly, then put the cars back in their boxes. 'I wasn't going to play Dinky toys,' he said.

'What are we going to play?' I asked.

'What I got for Christmas.'

He took us downstairs to the living room, and there beneath the big bay window was a Scalextric set.

It was the beginning of the end. Philip never came round to play again. Dennis did, but it wasn't the same.

'Do you want to play Dinky toys?' he'd say.

'Not really.'

'Me neither.'

We both began to dream of a Scalextric the way I imagined my father dreamed of an E-Type.

Of course he didn't buy an E-Type. But he didn't buy a Rover either. He went and bought another Hillman, blue and cream instead of cream and coffee.

'Is it automatic?' I said. An automatic would have a certain playground cachet.

'No. I decided against the automatic. Bit new-fangled.'

No one at school even knew we had a new car unless I told them. I didn't grumble. Our averageness was preserved.

Chapter 7

Taking it Easy
on the M6

My grandma didn't like my mother's Mini. She couldn't get in or out without help.

'It's too fiddly,' she said. 'You wouldn't see the Queen Mother in one of these.'

Taking her to the library was an operation. First a parking space no more than 50 yards away had to be found. Then Grandma would have to be hauled out of the car, helped up the steps of the library and a chair located for her. Then the book she wanted had to be hunted down; then she needed to be helped to the desk and restrained while she argued with the staff; then led back to the car.

It was a process, but all possible. Until they painted yellow *No Parking* lines outside the library.

It was going to happen sooner or later. There were simply too many cars clogging up the high street. 'Says here, car ownership has increased from two to ten million in the last ten years,' reported my father from behind the newspaper.

The road network was buckling under the numbers. Queues on trunk roads like the A30 became legendary and had folk songs written about them.

'Something has to be done,' said my father.

Something was done. The yellow lines were extended down the high street right past his office.

'Something has to be done about those yellow lines,' said my father.

The environment was beginning to suffer as well. Old market towns with narrow streets became gridlocked. The corners of medieval buildings were being knocked off as trucks barged through.

The huge increase in traffic also brought about a huge increase in accidents. In 1964 a staggering 7,000 people were killed on the roads. Without seat belts, drivers and passengers alike were flung through windows or mashed against dashboards. Elegant vehicles with Art Deco designs had edges so sharp they'd slice your legs off. An extremely relaxed attitude to speeding and drink-driving created scenes of carnage. Children were particularly at risk. Radical steps were needed. It was time to call for the enforcer. Tufty.

Cartoon squirrel Tufty Fluffytail was a crusader for the Royal Society for the Prevention of Accidents, on a mission to educate children in road safety. Parents enlisted their offspring in the Tufty Club and encouraged them to wear Tufty badges. We walked in line and sang the Tufty song. 'Stop, look and listen' became our mantra.

'The trouble with Tufty,' said Andrew at breakfast one day, 'is that he's a goody goody.'

'Tufty is very sensible,' said my mother.

'Tufty never leaves home without his mum,' said Andrew.

'What's wrong with that?'

'And he takes ten minutes to cross the road.'

It was true. Tufty and his mother would walk miles looking for a suitable crossing point and then take forever to go through their crossing-the-road check list. They looked left, then right, and left and right again, behind each other, up in the air and then left and right again, and then finally, just as they were about to cross, Tufty would say, 'Mummy, I can hear a lorry coming half a mile away.'

Tufty's problem was that he just wasn't the kind of kid you wanted to be friends with. 'I prefer Willy Weasel,' said Andrew, siding with Tufty's ne'er-do-well neighbour.

'Willy Weasel will get himself knocked over one day,' said my father.

Willy got himself knocked over every day. That was his role. While Tufty went shopping with his mummy to buy walking reins, Willy was hanging out by the bus stop, or 'playing in the road' as Tufty called it. Despite his scrapes with traffic Willy never learned. He was always back in the next story ready to be run over again. The message children got was that being knocked down was embarrassing, but you quickly got over it.

The day the yellow lines appeared outside the library my mother parked there as normal.

'What about these traffic wardens I've read about?' said Grandma.

'That's only in London.'

'They might be here on holiday.'

'We'll only be a minute.'

They were always more than a minute. We knew because we were made to wait in the car. Nothing happened that first time, and nothing happened the next time or the time after. Yellow lines, it seemed, were toothless. But the time after that a policeman pulled up on his bicycle.

He knocked on the window. 'Where's your mum or dad?'

We'd been warned what to do if this happened. 'In the library. My grandma's in there. Her legs aren't very good. She's on the toilet. They'll be out in a minute.'

The policeman started writing a ticket. My mother came out with Grandma just in time. 'You can't park here,' said the policeman.

'It's my mother, her legs aren't good.'

'There's nothing wrong with my legs,' said Grandma.

'Yellow lines are there for a reason,' said the policeman.

'My mother is 78 years old.'

'No I'm not...' Grandma stopped short. The policeman looked at her suspiciously.

'I'm 79,' she said.

He waived the ticket, and gave my mother a warning. 'Parked cars hinder traffic flow. Good traffic flow is essential.'

He was right. But poor traffic flow was a nationwide problem. The best way to improve it was to reduce the number of cars on the road. But that wasn't going to happen. As long ago as 1959 the Conservative Party had shown a family washing its Austin A35 on an election poster, and ever since a healthy motor manufacturing industry had been essential for economic progress. Cars were a sign of prosperity, of independence. Motorways were the way forward and successive governments invested heavily in roads. Forget about trains; trains were history. The government made sure of that when Ernest Marples, owner of the motorway-building company Marples Ridgway, was made Minister of Transport and promptly commissioned Dr Beeching to shut half the railway network.

One day, while my father worked in the garden, Mr Besant leaned over the fence and said, 'Want a tip?'

My father thought he was going to offer some guidance on dahlias, but he said: 'Buy shares in tarmac.'

Mr Besant knew what he was talking about. By 1964 there was an M1, M2, M4, M5 and M6. 'And what about the M3?' said my father. 'The one motorway that would do us some good and there's no sign of it.'

We felt snubbed. Motorways reached everywhere except the South and East Anglia. My father took it personally: 'I'm 36 and I've never driven on a motorway!'

If the motorway wouldn't come to us, we would have to go to the motorway. A letter came from my father's aunts in Warrington, enquiring when we were going to visit. They frequently asked this, safe in the knowledge that we never did, so they could come down to stay with us by the sea.

'Right, we'll show them,' said my father. And he got out his maps. 'We *will* visit, and what's more, we'll go on the motorway.'

To watch my father plan a long journey was to witness a ritual he perfected in his time as an RAF navigator. He lined up coloured pencils, rubbers, sharpeners. A map was spread out on the table and then a piece of foolscap was Sellotaped to a similarly sized piece of cardboard. Lines and columns were drawn. On the lines the towns we would pass through were listed. In the columns were road numbers, miles travelled, miles to go and miles since the last toilet break.

To get to Warrington we would head north on the A354 towards Blandford, and then take the A350 to Chippenham. The A429 took us through the Cotswolds to

Cirencester where a coffee break was pencilled in. From Cirencester we headed up through Worcester to Kidderminster; a route round Birmingham was plotted, bringing us to Stafford. 'And at Stafford we pick up the M6 motorway,' my father announced proudly, 'taking us all the way to Warrington. Do you realize what this means?'

'What?'

'Two less toilet breaks. The journey time will be halved!'

We packed as if we were heading off on a wagon train across the Western Plains. My mother put in blankets, pillows, first aid kit and picnic set. This was the longest car journey we had ever undertaken and my father went into a frenzy of checking and rechecking his levels. He even stuck a compass to the dashboard.

'What's that for?' I asked.

'We're heading north. The compass will always point to Warrington.'

I imagined us driving through fields, following the compass needle.

'Don't look so worried,' said my father. 'We're going on the motorway. It'll be a cruise.'

We set off at 7am. 'We're heading south,' said Andrew, his eyes on the compass.

'We're not out of the driveway yet,' said my father, reversing out.

We motored north. My six-year-old sister had learnt all the names of the cars from the Ladybird book and had become a keen car spotter. On short journeys it was amusing; on long journeys it was intolerable.

'Austin Cambridge.'

'Very good.'

'Sunbeam Alpine.'

'Yes, very good.'

'Ford Anglia.'

'Yes, all right.'

'Triumph Herald.'

'Will you shut up?'

We got to Cirencester. 'Coffee break. Tyre pressure check. Petrol,' announced my father.

We parked on the main street and went into a tea shop. 'Cirencester is an old Roman town with an interesting museum,' my father read from the tourist brochure.

'Let's visit it,' said my mother.

This was an outrageous suggestion. We were always told where the museums and places of historic interest were; they were always pointed out from the car. But we never went to visit them. The same thing happened in Tewkesbury, where we didn't get a look at the Abbey, and then in Worcester, where we didn't go to the porcelain museum. There was only one cultural highlight on this trip and that was the M6.

Signs for it began to appear past Wolverhampton. 'They seem to be sending us south,' said Andrew, still with his eyes on the compass.

'You're right,' said my father and, trusting his own home-made directions rather than the signs the Ministry of Transport had gone to great trouble to erect, he headed north.

This took us on back roads instead of the signposted ones. But then, as we browed a hill, my father cried: 'Look, there it is!'

In the distance, we could see it. A corridor cut into the landscape, and a smooth, black curve running away between the low hills. My father leant forward in his seat, a sure sign he was excited. We could see the cars now, speeding by effortlessly: no interruptions, no twists in the road, no hint of congestion. The whole thing looked streamlined and elegant.

But then, as we reached it, we passed straight underneath, the motorway crossing our road on an overpass.

'What's happening?' said my father.

'We're heading east now,' said Andrew.

'We've gone under it,' said my mother.

'Yes I know we've gone under it.'

He stopped the car firmly and did a three-point turn, then went back to the overpass. The traffic boomed overhead, but there was no way of getting on the motorway. He got out of the car and stood there looking around. There must be an entrance somewhere. There was a field with a gate and he looked over that to see if there was a way on, but there was nothing.

'How strange,' he said when he came back. He studied the map. 'We'll try further up.'

'We're heading west now,' said Andrew.

'Yes, yes.'

We drove round more country roads. We lost view of the motorway.

'Do you want me to navigate?' asked my mother.

'Quite all right, thank you.' But he was using his tense voice, the one he used when things weren't quite all right at all.

We reached the motorway again. This time we went over it on a bridge.

'Oh bloody hell!' said my father.

'No need for that!' said my mother.

'This is a motorway, and we can't get on the bloody thing.'

He turned round and headed off again.

'Heading north now,' said Andrew.

'Just shut up, all right?'

'Ford Prefect,' said my sister.

'I said shut up!'

We drove off again, driving parallel with the motorway, watching the cars zoom past us.

'This is nice countryside,' said my mother.

My father chewed on his pipe stem until bits of plastic broke off.

We had two more attempts. Call us naïve country folk, but we just hadn't heard of junctions and on-ramps. The idea of two roads meeting and there being no interchange was something that was just too difficult to comprehend.

Eventually we stumbled across a big roundabout. 'Sign there says the M6,' said my mother.

'Thank God for that!'

It was an on-ramp at last, and my father steered up it and then there we were, motoring with the rest of the fashionable people along the M6. My father quickly regained his composure, pleased with himself. He was part of the motorway revolution at last. 'Cuts the journey time in half you know.'

'We're heading south now,' said Andrew.

'We can't be. This is the M6.'

'Compass says we're heading south.'

'The M6 goes south to north,' said my father.

'It also goes north to south,' said my mother.

'Oh buggeration!' he said as he realized his fundamental mistake, and he lost his composure just as quickly as he had regained it.

We drove all the way back to Stafford to the previous exit and finally found the ramp heading north.

'I'm going to write to the Minister of Transport about this.'

'I'm sure he'll be delighted to hear from you,' said my mother.

Driving on the motorway was a thrill. For about five minutes. We quickly got up to 60 miles an hour, but with everyone travelling at that speed, it soon felt like 30. There were no views, and not much traffic. Just miles and miles of motorway, and my father trying to keep us amused with trivia: 'Did you know that birds follow motorways as a navigational aid?' He knew a lot more about motorways than he did about the Roman occupation.

'What's this thing coming up?' said my mother.

'It's a service area.'

'Good. We can go to the toilet.'

'No, we can't.'

'Why not?'

'Because there's not a toilet break for another 30 minutes. That's the whole idea.'

'You daughter needs to go to the toilet.'

'No she doesn't. She can hang on.' My father was very proud of the Wallington bladders and liked to test them.

But there was no way he was going to be allowed to drive past a motorway service station. My mother had heard about these places on TV. They had hot air hand dryers and you spotted film stars there. They were on a par with airport departure lounges.

In the car park she put on her make-up and smacked her lips, then swapped her car shoes for heels.

'We're only going to be a minute,' said my father.

The restaurant was in the bridge over the motorway, so you could sit there and watch the traffic speed past below. It didn't take long to realize that the service stations were much more fun than the motorways themselves.

A waitress came and took our order for tea and fruit cake.

'Look, is that Dirk Bogarde over there?' said my mother.

We all spun round. There was a man at a table with jet black hair and a pocket handkerchief.

'Looks nothing like Dirk Bogarde,' said my father.

My mother bought postcards of the motorway and sent them to all her friends. She even sent one to her hairdressers: 'Here we are, taking it easy on the M6.'

My sister looked out of the window and called out: 'Vauxhall Vesta. Vauxhall Vesta. Vauxhall Vesta, Vauxhall Vesta, Vauxhall Vesta, Vauxhall Vesta.'

'What are you talking about?' said my father.

'It's a car transporter,' said Andrew.

'Don't look,' whispered my mother, 'but that woman's the spitting image of Diana Dors.'

The aunts were pleased to see us. They said we were their first visitors since the war. My father tried to thrill them with stories of motorway travel: 'We went 68 miles an hour!' But they were more interested in the price of fruit cake in the service area.

The three of them lived together in a big house with a grandfather clock that had a very loud tick and a deafening chime. In the garage was something rather more interesting: a vehicle under a dust sheet. My father whipped it off and there stood a Morris 1000. It belonged to Aunt Nora but: 'The doctor has told her to stop driving,' said Aunt May.

Nora was on strong medication. Her mental health wasn't good and social services were keeping an eye on her. She hadn't been the same since she saw the Pope on the garage roof.

'Which Pope?' asked my father.

'She didn't say,' said Aunt May. 'Pius XII or John XXIII, I imagine.'

None of the other aunts drove and so the car hadn't been out since Nora's final foray when she mounted the kerb in town and hit the wall outside the post office.

'You almost killed my wife!' a man had shouted at her.

'I was only lighting a cigarette,' Nora had explained.

We inspected the damage the wall had done, a big dent and a buckled wing. 'Superficial,' said my father.

Inside, the car smelt of the crammed ashtray, and there were little burn marks dotted around the upholstery where Nora had dropped her butts.

My father checked the Morris's levels and started the engine. It jumped into life first time; it sounded full of energy.

'We'll take her down to the garage and put some air in the tyres,' he said.

The Morris motored happily through town. I was 12 years old. I didn't know it, but I was sitting in the car in which I would learn to drive.

Chapter 8

What I Did
on My Holidays

A new car usually meant a new baby. One day my father brought home a two-tone blue and white Morris Oxford. Sure enough, a few months later my mother brought home another brother.

The Morris Oxford was big, a proper family car with a big face and a big arse. The back seat was wide enough for three children to sit comfortably: me on one side, brother Andrew on the other and sister Jane in the middle with her legs not touching the floor. The new baby was up front as usual on mother's lap.

I've got an old cine-camera film of us all on a picnic in the Purbeck Hills. There we are with a blanket laid out, crisps everywhere, Thermos flask and biscuits, the creamy Dorset scenery stretching away and the shiny new Morris Oxford framed in the background. My mother is sitting with baby Jonathan. My brother and sister and I are playing cricket with my father. He's bowling – those really annoying spinners none of us could hit. Then he's batting. Then he's still batting and still batting. He keeps giving us dolly catches, but we keep dropping them.

Then the boot of the Morris is open and everything is being piled inside. My brother is scowling; my father has his pipe at a serious angle. Words have been said. Then we're all happy again, because the car is parked and we're picking blackberries by the roadside, juice smeared over my sister's face. Then there's a shot of us driving home, my mother pointing the camera out of the window, the view of the coastline stretching west to Portland Bill.

They were the days childhood memories are made of. My father never happier than when he was driving; my mother never more satisfied than when she had found a good picnic spot; kids fighting and laughing, never still. The Morris Oxford one of the family, ever dependable.

And then came the bombshell.

One day my mother said, 'I'm sorry. I'm bored with all the picnic spots round here.'

We looked at her as if she'd just announced she was leaving with a tall man in a Ford Consul.

But then she added: 'I think we need to go abroad.'

My father didn't look up from his newspaper.

But that night he got out his pencils and sharpeners, his rubbers and his rulers, and he stayed up until the small hours. When I sneaked a look at his work the following morning I saw a new chart, but with place names I'd never heard of and certainly couldn't pronounce. Instead of Cirencester and Chippenham it was Limoges, Toulouse and Perpignan, and on the map the red line of the route went ever south, down and down through France and over the border into Spain.

'The Costa Brava is a beautifully undeveloped coastal region. Fishing villages and cheerful locals. The perfect family holiday destination.' So said Mr Pilling who ran an off licence in town and was keen to rent out his villa. It sounded fine to us. The trip to Warrington had awakened our sense of adventure. We booked a fortnight in August.

Andrew practised his Spanish. '*Pásame la mantequilla.*'

'What does that mean?' said my mother.

'Pass the butter.'

'You're going to be very useful on this holiday,' said my father.

We were all excited for different reasons: Andrew to try out his Spanish; me because on the last day of term my teacher had commissioned the class to write an essay, 'What I did on my holidays,' and I knew I would have the best story; and my mother because she saw the journey as a picnicker's paradise. For her the drive through France would be one orgy of picnic food, eaten on rugs in vineyards with a château on one side and a medieval town on the other: cheeses, hams, French sticks, fresh figs. Not a jar of Marmite in sight.

My father was delighted because he had discovered that as tourists in France we would be given vouchers for cheap fuel. His joy was tempered when he discovered that French tourists got the same deal over here. But he was enthusiastic about the whole continental experience and he prepared in an even more meticulous fashion than usual. He even decided to involve Mr Goodall.

'Here, put a tiger in your tank,' said Mr Goodall, giving us a tiger tail on a string, the latest Esso promotion.

'What happened to "The Esso sign means happy motoring"?' said my father.

'We've moved on from there,' said Mr Goodall.

'What are we supposed to do with this?' said my father, examining his tiger tail.

'Hang it round your rear-view mirror.'

'Why?'

'I haven't got a clue.'

When we told him of our holiday plans he shook his head. 'You don't want to go over there, Mr Wallington.'

'Why not?'

'I was at Dunkirk; I know what it's like.'

Mr Goodall's attitude was extreme but not unusual. Travelling abroad was still considered by many to be intrepid; driving there the activity of the irresponsible.

'One thing's for sure,' said Mr Goodall, 'you don't want to break down,' and he took it upon himself to provide us with a breakdown kit. He made a list of the problems the Morris might have on a 2,000-mile trip, and supplied a box of spares for every eventuality. In it were plugs and pipes, hoses and fan belts, fluids and filters, plus a set of tools so extensive we could have stopped in the middle of France and set up a garage.

'And you absolutely must have headlight beam reflectors,' said Mr Goodall, 'otherwise the French lorry drivers will drive straight at you and force you off the road. So I've heard.'

By the time all the equipment was on board there was little room for anything else.

'You need a roof rack,' said Mr Goodall.

'Good idea,' said my father.

'I can sell you one. Double Green Shield Stamps.'

We left one evening at the beginning of August. We piled into the car like astronauts leaving Earth, except we weren't strapped in. 'All set?' said my father.

'All set,' said my mother.

'I think we'll just say a little prayer to St Christopher,' he said.

We joined hands and put our heads down, and in the time it took us to mutter three Hail Marys, what had started off as an exciting, but pretty straightforward, car ride to sunny Spain had become an expedition into the wilderness from which we might never return.

My father started the engine, then turned it off. 'Forgot one thing,' he said and ran back into the house. He came back with a packet of bacon.

'You're not taking your own bacon?'

'I've heard bad stories about foreign bacon.'

He handed it to me in a Tupperware tub. 'Put that somewhere cool.'

Weymouth Docks wasn't really equipped for car ferries. Having said that, the ferry wasn't really equipped for cars. They might have had drive-on and drive-off facilities at some of the flashier ports like Dover, but in Weymouth you parked on the quay and boarded the boat, then watched from the deck as a docker drove your vehicle into a net which was then hoisted up and lowered into the ship's hold. We held our breath as our dear Morris Oxford, its underbelly showing for all to see, was swung through the air. '*Usted ha estacionado en el pie*,' said Andrew.

'What does that mean?'

'You have parked on my foot.'

The ferry was like a troop ship. Once on board men and women were segregated: my father, Andrew and I slept in the men's bunks. I lay awake as the ship's engines churned beneath me, so desperately excited to be heading abroad for the first time. My father got into conversation with a man from Swindon. They were both very proud of themselves for taking their families on a continental trip. Mr Swindon and his wife were going to the Dordogne. He was driving a Cortina. My father went through the list of spares he had brought, and Mr Swindon grew more and more anxious.

'You mean you don't have a spare carburettor?' said my father.

'They've got garages in France,' said Mr Swindon.

'You can't be too careful,' said my father.

For the first time I wondered if, in fact, you *could* be too careful.

We drove south for almost three days. My father smoked his pipe from Saint-Malo to Perpignan. 'Helps me concentrate,' he said.

That first morning we weren't allowed to make a noise: 'Ssh, your father's trying to drive on the right.' But slowly, as he grew more confident, he relaxed, and after four hours he even granted us a toilet break.

We saw other British cars on the road, but so few that we'd flash lights and honk horns. We three sat on the back seat with no radio, no music. We had windows to entertain ourselves and we played I Spy in French. 'Something beginning with V.' '*Vache*?' 'No.' '*Voiture*?' 'Yes.'

We headed into deepest France. We discovered yoghurt. The first night we stayed at a strange roadside inn called Hôtel de la Gare, strange because it was surrounded by fields with no sign of a station anywhere. We were the only guests. My diary notes they served us very thick potato soup, and a meat dish that so impressed my father he poured a glass of wine and said to the waitress, '*Pour le chef.*'

A bemused chef came out from the kitchen, looking as though he'd never had a compliment in his life before.

'*Me gustaría un flan con nata,*' said Andrew.

'What's that mean?'

'I would like some pudding with cream.'

The next day we got close to the Spanish border. The Morris Oxford was doing just fine. With its GB sticker and loaded roof rack it looked intrepid. My father kept a constant check on its levels and pressures and made notes in his logbook. The other thing he noted was menu prices. When we'd all gone to bed he would go for a stroll round town and look in restaurant windows.

'Why do you look at menus?' said my mother.

'They relax me,' and he got out his logbook and read to us: '*Boeuf aux champignons F8,50. Canard à l'orange F9,00. Mousse au chocolat F2,40,*' until we fell asleep.

The following morning we crossed into Spain in a thunderstorm, then drove down to the Costa Brava. Mr Pilling hadn't lied. It was indeed unspoilt and undeveloped. It was warm and sunny and the English were respected by the whole village because we'd just won the World Cup.

'Bobby Moore.'

'Bobby Charlton.'

My diary notes of the time in Spain are sparse. I had imagined something incredibly exciting was going to happen to me to bring my essay alive, but we did little except go to the beach. Despite travelling two thousand miles to a foreign place we did exactly as we did at home. Perhaps the most intriguing thing about Spain was that as soon as we got there my brother refused to speak any more Spanish.

We all tried the Spanish equivalent of bacon, but weren't impressed. My father refused to share his and we could hardly blame him. 'First rule of continental travel,' he said, as he expertly read the English papers in the newsagents without taking them out of the rack, 'come properly prepared. You'll know next time.'

He was about to find out just how right he was.

Two weeks passed in a flash. Soon we were packing up the car and heading back over the border. We made good time up through France and on the second day we were near Tours, with plenty of time to get to Saint-Malo and the night boat back to Weymouth.

'We're near the Loire Valley,' said my mother. She'd been told this was the El Dorado of picnic sites. She saw us having our last meal sitting in the shade of poplar trees with the river running easily by our side, a gentle breeze making the grass bend, a field of sunflowers lighting up the opposite bank.

My father was already in a poor mood. That morning he'd stopped at a petrol station to use up the last of his fuel coupons. As he went to the kiosk my mother gave him some postcards and asked him to see if he could find a box.

When he returned he was shaking with anger.

'What happened?' said my mother.

He put his head on the wheel and made a noise like a charging bull.

'Was there a post box?'

'Yes.'

'Did you post my cards?'

'No. I posted the petrol coupons.'

'What did you do with my cards?'

'I tried to pay for the petrol with them.'

We motored on in silence for the rest of the morning. But now it was lunchtime and we were all hungry. 'Turn left here,' said my mother.

'Why?'

'I can sense a perfect picnic site.'

He scowled. 'Half an hour, max.'

He turned left down a country road that took us through lavender fields. 'Turn next right,' said my mother, 'and we'll be at the river.'

My father turned right and we found ourselves in a tyre dump.

'Oh dear,' she said.

'I want my picnic now,' said my sister.

'You can't have a picnic here,' said my mother.

'Why not?' said my father, who quite liked the idea of having his lunch surrounded by tyres.

'*Me gustaría un sándwich de huevo,*' said Andrew who had found his Spanish tongue again, but no one was interested in what he was saying any more.

We pressed on, climbing above the river. 'Where the hell are you taking us?' said my father, his temper easily rising.

But there was no reasoning with my mother by this stage. She could sense something special just round the corner.

'I can see the river. Almost there,' she said.

Suddenly, my father stiffened as if he'd been shot.

He tapped one of the gauges on the Morris's dashboard, the one marked 'Temp'. The needle was swinging steadily into the red.

He paled and brought the car to a stop. Steam was rising from the bonnet.

'What's the matter?' said my mother.

'We've overheated.'

'What does that mean?'

'It means we've broken down!' he snapped.

'Can't we just make it down to the river...?'

'No!'

He was already out of the car and lifting the bonnet. Steam poured out. It quickly cleared and he peered at the engine. You can tell a man who knows about engines just by the way he peers at them, and my father knew little about engines.

He was thinking out loud: 'Steam. That means it must be overheating. That means the radiator isn't doing its job.'

'*No hay agua*,' said Andrew.

'What?'

'No water.'

'Exactly. No water.' He twisted the radiator cap. 'Stand back!' he cried, even though the rest of us were already stood well back and tucking into ham and a French stick.

He lifted the cap and steam shot up into the china blue sky.

'Has that fixed it?' said my mother.

'No.'

'Thought it might be like lancing a boil.'

'No water in the radiator, so...'

'*Hay una fuga*.'

'Will you stop speaking in bloody Spanish?'

Andrew zipped his mouth shut.

'There must be a leak,' said my father. He just had to find out where. He traced the radiator pipes back until he found the fault. A hose had split near the join with the engine block. It would need to be replaced.

'Excellent,' said my father.

'Have you fixed it?'

'No. But I'm going to. Bring me the box of spare parts.' He knew he had a spare hose. Mr Goodall wouldn't have dreamed of letting us leave the country without a spare set of hoses.

He rummaged through the box until he found them; somewhere among them was the one he was looking for.

No it wasn't. There were all different sizes, all different shapes, but not the one he needed. It was then he looked at the packet and realized the hoses weren't for a Morris Oxford.

Now steam came out of my father. He swore so badly my mother started to shout at him. I started to argue with my brother. My sister started to tease two-year-old Jonathan. In minutes all the underlying tensions of a two-thousand-mile family car journey surfaced in textbook fashion. My father said something unforgivable. My mother burst into tears. I ate my brother's yoghurt and got a thump for it. Jonathan decided to make a break for home and set off toddling towards Saint-Malo.

My mother announced she was leaving and dragged us all off down the road with her. 'Well if you ever want to get out of here, find some water!' shouted my father after us.

We left him hunched over the bonnet, swearing loudly at Mr Goodall and his garage and his family.

We walked in the afternoon heat, my mother carrying baby Jonathan, my sister eating a French stick. 'There'll be water in the River Loire,' I said to my mother. She wasn't interested.

But there was no sign of the river now, just more vineyards, and the dry and cracked earth.

'This shouldn't be happening,' said Jane. 'We prayed to St Christopher after all.'

'There's a farmhouse over there,' said Andrew.

'See,' I said, 'St Christopher has sent us a farmhouse.'

'Why didn't he just send us a hose that fit?' said Andrew.

'St Christopher works in funny ways,' said my mother and marched us all up the drive.

A duck answered the door; behind it stood a woman. With her childhood French and many hand gestures my mother explained our vehicle had broken down and she had to get back to England because she needed to get a divorce. The woman shook her head in sympathy, then called out for her husband. A man appeared with soup stains down his shirt. He piled us into his pick-up and took us back down the road.

When we got back to my father he was kneeling on the road attacking the hoses with a hacksaw to try and make one fit. 'We're going to miss the boat now,' he raged. 'We're going to miss the boat.' He sounded delirious.

My mother translated these fears to the farmer. He didn't hesitate and tied a rope to the front of the Morris. We just accepted what he was doing and all jumped back in the car.

'Where's he taking us?' said my father.

My mother wasn't speaking to him.

He towed us back to the main road. 'Maybe he's going

to take us all the way to the boat,' said Andrew. Soon, though, we turned into a garage. There, a mechanic took one look at the radiator and another at the hose and started to laugh. The farmer started to laugh. My father pretended to laugh. Then the mechanic went inside and came out with another hose, which he slipped onto the pipe with ease. He tightened it up and filled the radiator with water and we were done.

My father went from despair to euphoria. He shook everyone's hand. He paid the mechanic and tipped him generously. He slipped the farmer something for his trouble. If he'd had any bacon left he would have handed it over. Instead he took two bottles of wine from the boot and offered them as a small token, just as he had handed the chef a glass at the Hôtel de la Gare. '*Pour le mechanic.*'

'Bobby Charlton,' said the mechanic.

'Bobby Moore,' said the farmer.

We drove to Saint-Malo in silence. At one point my father put his hand out and patted my mother's knee in apology. She brushed it away. He sighed his sigh that said: 'Oh, the loneliness of command.'

We got home and told everyone our holiday stories: how interesting the drive through France was; how colourful life in Spain could be; how sunny and friendly the Costa Brava was. At first we were reluctant to tell the tale of the breakdown. I think we all felt a little bit embarrassed. I was 13 years old and shocked at the way our seemingly indestructible family unit had disintegrated in a flash.

But eventually we started to talk about it and smile, and then we discovered that it was the part of the holiday that friends enjoyed hearing about the most. So much so that my father told it again and again, embellishing it more each time: making the breakdown more severe, his temper more foul, the family argument more comic; the farmer had a beret and a big moustache; the drive to the boat was a hair-raising race through Normandy, and we got to the quay just as they were untying the ropes.

The story became legendary and I made it the focus of my 'What I did on my holidays' essay.

'Very good,' said my teacher, and I knew then that no one wants to hear about the nice things that happen to you on holiday. Misfortune, be it stomach bugs, bad weather, motoring breakdowns or, best of all, family falling out is much more interesting.

My father went to see Mr Goodall and expected him to wriggle with remorse. He apologized in the only way he knew, by giving us a box of 'Put a Tiger in Your Tank' badges.

He was more concerned when he discovered that we had let a French mechanic work on our car. 'I'll give it a good check over. They don't know what they're doing over there.'

Chapter 9

None of the Above

Aunt Nora died. Against all the odds it was a heart attack that killed her rather than a house fire started by one of her cigarette ends. The other aunts immediately announced they were down-sizing. They told my father he could have any furniture he wanted. They also told him he could have Nora's Morris 1000.

'Your mother and I have had a talk and decided you can have the car for your birthday,' he said to me.

'OK,' I said, in the nonchalant way you do when you're coming up to 17 and someone says, 'Do you want a car?'

My father went up to Warrington to pick it up. It was the only time I ever knew him take a train anywhere. It was while he was gone that the enormity of what was about to happen to me sunk in. My life would change. I would be mobile. I could drive along smoking a cigarette with one arm hanging out of the window. Girls would be all over me.

My father drove the Morris 1000 down from Warrington without any trouble. He did have one shock though, when he went to fill up with petrol near Chester. 'You operated the pump yourself. A self-service garage. Can you believe it?'

He arrived home with the grandfather clock somehow wedged into the car.

'How have you managed to fit that in?' said my mother.

'The front seat folds down,' he said. 'It's almost like a bed.'

This just got better and better. All I needed to do was pass my driving test.

The Morris 1000 wasn't an attractive car. It looked like a cartoon version of itself. But it had an endearing nature. Who could resist its indicator mechanism? You flicked a stalk on the steering wheel and an illuminated yellow arrow popped out of the side of the car. It was hard not to sit in the garage and just play with it.

The folding seat was its best feature though. I lounged in the back and imagined I was out on my first date. I made a list of all the things I'd need: cushions, blanket, radio, contraceptives, tin of humbugs. I arranged myself and tried to work out just how the seduction process would work. My mother caught me. 'What are you doing?'

'Polishing the leather.'

'Your Aunt Nora would be very pleased.'

As usual my father offered to be instructor.

'No, no, you're too busy,' I said. 'I'll have lessons from El Passo.' The age of the punning driving school was already upon us. Lucky Brake, Passed It and El Passo had pushed stuffy East Dorset Motoring School aside.

'Lessons are expensive. And besides.'

'Besides what?'

'We need to talk.'

'About what...?'

'All sorts of things.'

I quizzed my brother, whom my father had also taught. I said, 'What does "We need to talk" mean?'

'It means sex.'

'What!'

'He teaches you to drive and gives you sexual advice.'

It was hard to believe. The mention of the word 'sex' made my father blush, particularly if any of his children were around. Whenever a sexy scene came on *The Wednesday Play* he sent me out to make tea.

'Why does he want to talk about sex when he's teaching you to drive?'

'Driving and sex have a lot in common in his view of the world.'

They did in mine as well. Everyone in my sixth form was convinced that a driving licence and virginity were inextricably linked: if you gained the former you lost the latter. The implication was that this was straightforward. But something told me it was never going to be so simple. Passing your driving test was plain enough: you needed some skill, some application and a certain amount of luck. Losing your virginity had similarities, but there was one big difference: you needed someone to lose your virginity with.

I did actually have someone in mind. Although I hadn't been polite enough to tell her yet. Her name was Mandy and she had a Saturday job as a market researcher. She would stand in the way of passers-by on the high street, and ask them if they would kindly accompany her into the Town Hall and answer a few questions about liver sausage, or whatever product she was marketing that weekend. Most people would try to avoid her, but I made it my business to bump into her. She only had to say the word and I was accompanying her up the steps into the Town Hall. There she'd put a tray of liver sausage on Ritz crackers before me. I'd sample them and she'd say, 'Do you think Moffit's liver sausage is a) delicious, b) tasty, but not that tasty, c) unpleasant, or d) none of the above?'

'Er...' and I'd look into her eyes and know there was only one answer. 'A.'

'Delicious. Thank you very much for your help.'

'You're welcome.'

'Anything else I can sample?'

'That's all thanks.'

The seduction process seemed to me to be an escalation of five stages. I was stuck at the liver sausage stage, which could only be stage one.

I tied L plates onto the Morris. 'Lesson one,' said my father. 'How to fill up with petrol.'

He drove me to Mr Goodall. 'You're not 17!?' he said to me and patted me on the head. 'I remember you in your pram.' It's what he had said to my brother when he put L plates on, and what he would say to my sister.

My father told him about the self-service petrol station he'd encountered driving back from Warrington. Mr Goodall shook his head in disbelief. If you so much as touched the pump on his forecourt he'd have you in an arm-lock and be on the phone to the police.

'It won't catch on,' said Mr Goodall, and gave me a World Cup 1970 commemorative coin, featuring Jeff Astle.

My father drove me to the site of a demolished

brickworks, a big, flattened expanse where we drove round in circles all morning getting to know the basics. I was very nervous, not because of the driving, but because I thought at any moment he might say something like: 'Don't grip the steering wheel so tightly, try and imagine you've got a pretty girl in your arms,' and before I knew it he'd be giving me tips on how to undo a bra.

But he said nothing on the subject of sex. He just talked about clutch control and finding the biting point. Only at the end of the lesson did he say something out of character: 'The thing about learning to drive is it gives you independence. You're a free man.'

It was unlike him to say something emotional. He dealt in definites; he disliked concepts that couldn't be tested with a dipstick. But sitting in the instructor's seat was letting a different side of him emerge. Instead of being tense and quick to blame, as he no doubt was when he tried to teach my mother, he was calm and relaxed and understanding, even when I made basic mistakes, like hitting a dustbin on the pavement when I attempted a three-point turn.

'Easily done,' he said as we picked up rubbish from the kerb.

On Saturday I went into town again and presented myself to Mandy. She took me into the Town Hall as usual and asked me to smell soap. 'Do you think Apple Blossom soap smells a) exotic, b) okay, but nothing special, c) it stinks, or d) none of the above?'

'Er... I think it smells erotic.'

'I said exotic.'

'Yeah, that's it.'

'Thank you very much for your help.'

'You're welcome.'

She looked back at her clipboard. I didn't know what to do so I tossed my car keys in my hand.

She glanced at me. 'Have you got a car?'

'Yes.'

She nodded. The look in her eye suggested she was either impressed and waiting to be asked out for a drive, or she felt sorry for me. I couldn't tell which. 'I haven't passed my test yet though,' I said.

'Our house is on the corner where all the learner drivers practise their reversing.'

She was telling me where she lived. I reckoned that was escalation to stage three right there.

She laughed. 'Sometimes they come through the hedge.'

At last, a way of meeting her without her clipboard.

My father gave me a lesson every Thursday evening. 'Better than watching *Top of the Pops*, eh?'

I kept waiting for the sex talk but it never came. Then one evening, after we'd done hill starts and emergency stops, he said, 'You need to learn your Highway Code. If you go to the bookcase in our bedroom you'll find a copy on the top shelf.'

Of course. This was his ploy. He was directing me to where I would find the sex manuals: *The Joy of Sex*, the *Karma Sutra*, a dog-eared copy of *Fanny Hill*.

But no. I went to the top shelf as directed and there I found the Highway Code.

But then I thought: maybe 'code' is the operative word here; the Highway Code is in fact a metaphor for good sexual practice. The art of adjusting the seat and mirror was foreplay. A good emergency stop was contraception. An accurate three-point turn was... I didn't know what a three-point turn was, but it sounded pretty advanced.

Things were suddenly clearer. When he talked about the need to find the biting point he could easily have been referring to that tricky part of the seduction routine when everything was in the balance, and how it was important not to get overexcited. I made a note. What a clever old dog he was.

He found out the route round town that the examiners took candidates on, and decided we should have a rehearsal. We found the place where they tested three-point turns and I executed one perfectly. The same with emergency stops. But when we got to the spot where they tested reversing round a corner I went to pieces. This was the corner on which Mandy lived.

I went up the kerb and into the hedge.

'I think we'd better get out of here quick,' said my father.

But then there was Mandy striding down her driveway towards us.

'So sorry,' said my father. 'We were all learners once.'

'It's you,' said Mandy.

'Hi.'

'Listen,' she said. 'It's very easy. I'll be a marker on the kerb right here,' and she stood like a bollard on the pavement. 'As soon as you see me in your rear-view mirror, give it the right-hand-down.'

She stood there as I tried again. And as I looked into the mirror there she was, waving, willing me on. I swung the wheel and performed the manoeuvre expertly. 'Perfect,' she called.

It was all the encouragement I needed. After the lesson I said to my father: 'I'm ready for my test.'

I applied and was given a Tuesday afternoon four weeks away. I ringed it in red on the calendar. The Saturday before, I saw Mandy in town as usual. This week she was marketing shampoo, and we discussed how many times a week I washed my hair. Such an intimate conversation convinced me I had moved to the stage where I needed to take action. I said, 'If I were to ask you out to *Butch Cassidy and the Sundance Kid* on Tuesday night would you say a) no, I've already seen it, b) all right, unless something better comes up, c) sure, pick me up at seven-thirty, or d) none of the above?'

She thought about it a moment.

'D.'

'None of the above?'

'Pick me up at eight o'clock.'

Things were slipping neatly into place. But I couldn't get complacent. My brother had just told me about a Chinese space rocket that was going to crash land somewhere, the middle of the following week.

'So?'

'No one knows where it's going to land.'

'It'll land in the ocean. They always do.'

'It could just as easily land on Woolworths. Or this house.'

He was right. The odds were against it, but I couldn't take chances. If I didn't pass my test it meant I might die a virgin. I stuck my head deep into the Highway Code.

My father gave me one last lesson, and he wanted to talk about anything other than learning to drive. He said, 'Only seems like yesterday we were in the old Ford coming back from the hospital with you, and now look at you. Size 10 feet.'

'I thought the story was you didn't have the Ford in time.'

'Yes I did. It came the day they climbed Everest.'

'I was born before that.'

'Are you sure?'

'Positive.'

'Whatever, remember that time we went to see Aunt Monica and we couldn't stop and you had to pee in a milk bottle on the back seat?'

'No, I don't remember that.'

I began to realize what all this was about. As far as he was concerned a driving test was the exam that marked the end of childhood. After this I was an adult.

'Once you've got your licence you'll probably want to leave home,' he said.

I had no intention of leaving home.

'A driving licence is as good as a passport. You can go to Australia if you want.'

But it sounded like leaving home might be compulsory.

I drove appallingly that evening. All I could think about was Mandy, and the Chinese rocket falling to earth. My father was unruffled. 'I notice you signalled left then and turned right.'

'An easy mistake.'

'The examiner might think differently.'

Then when I did a three-point turn I hit a dustbin on the pavement again.

'Not quite yourself this evening.'

'No.'

'Anything I can help with?'

'I'm just a bit... well...'

'Is a woman involved?'

'Yes.'

'Is it that one who stands in the high street handing out Moffit's liver sausage on crackers?'

'Yes.'

'Very tasty.'

I never found out if he was referring to the liver sausage or Mandy.

I got up early and cleaned the car, then we went to fill up with petrol. 'Good luck,' said Mr Goodall, and gave me another World Cup coin. 'You've given me Jeff Astle again. That's five Jeff Astles I've got.'

'Good player, Jeff Astle.'

We drove to Poole and waited outside the test centre.

'How many times did you take your test?' I asked my father.

He was silent for a moment. He looked up as if he was scanning the sky for the Chinese rocket. He said, 'I learnt to drive during the war. There were no driving instructors. You just learnt.'

'So how many times?'

'You just applied for a provisional licence and then after a certain period of time... well, they gave you a full one.'

'Are you saying you never took a driving test?'

'No I didn't.'

I went and sat in the reception with the other examinees and wondered if my father was a virgin when he got married.

A friend from school was across the room. He said, 'I just hope I don't get the Major.'

'Who's the Major?'

'He's a nightmare. He fails everyone.'

As he spoke, out of the office came a man wearing cavalry twill trousers, a khaki shirt, a sports jacket and regimental tie.

My friend stiffened. The Major said: 'Mr Wallington.'

I looked round the room in the hope there was another Mr Wallington taking his test that day, but there wasn't.

I thought I did fine. I got the hand signals all right. I'm pretty sure my hill start was adequate, and when I reversed round the corner I lined up the lamppost as Mandy had taught me to and executed it perfectly. I didn't hit any dustbins. I knew my Highway Code. The only problem came when I looked in the mirror and there on the back seat saw myself sprawled with Mandy in an embrace so tight and passionate I may have been distracted and gone straight across a junction.

Back at the test centre the Major wrote up his notes, ripped off a piece of paper from his pad and handed it to me. I was so sure I was going to pass I couldn't really comprehend what he meant when he said, 'I have to tell you you've failed your driving test for reasons given on this form,' and he glanced at me with a look that said he knew very well the only reason I wanted a licence was so

I could fold the seat down and get up to no good.

Experience had told the Major not to hang around in the car if you failed the candidate, and so moving remarkably swiftly for a man of his build he was quickly out and I was on my own. I wanted to bang my head on the dashboard and wake myself up. I put my hands up to my face. The door opened. It had to be the Major come back to tell me he'd made a mistake.

But it was my father. He sat down in the passenger seat. 'You got the Major.'

'Yes.'

'The Major fails everyone first time. I wouldn't worry about it.'

Back home my brother consoled me. 'The good news is the Chinese rocket is heading for Siberia.'

'What was all that about driving and advice on sex?'

'You didn't believe me did you?'

That evening I walked round to Mandy's house.

'I thought you had a car,' she said.

'I failed my test.'

'Hard luck.'

'What do you want to do?'

'I thought we were going to the cinema.'

'I'll need to have my father in the passenger seat.'

'I can sit in your passenger seat.'

'You've not...'

'Yes I have.'

'You've... why didn't you say?'

'You never asked.'

We went to see *Butch Cassidy*. Other couples in the cinema were all over each other, but Mandy and I sat with arms folded. This was only stage four after all.

On the way home we parked in the Municipal Golf Club car park. We sat and looked at the stars.

'Look, there's the Belt of Orion,' I said.

'I like this car.'

'And there's the snare of the plough.'

'Does that seat fold down?'

'And that's either a shooting star or part of the Chinese rocket crashing to earth.'

'Where?'

'You can see it better in the back seat.'

The back seat of the Morris was as seductive as a four-poster bed, which was something the manufacturers never mentioned in advertisements. Stage five was achieved, and although it was all a bit out of control to begin with – 'Are you feeling a) aroused and confident, b) aroused but clumsy, c) not aroused, or d) none of the above?'... 'B.' ... 'Me too' – I found that if you visited the Golf Club car park enough times over the course of a summer things quickly improved.

I found the biting point.

My father decided he wouldn't teach me any more. It was time to have proper driving lessons. I took a short course from El Passo, and failed again. It didn't seem important as long as I had Mandy in the passenger seat.

England lost the World Cup. Jeff Astle missed an open goal. Eventually I did pass my test, but by that time Mandy and I had parted. She went away to university and never asked me my feelings on shampoo or cheese slices again.

The day I passed my test I snipped the L plates off the Morris and sat in the driver's seat unaccompanied for the first time. I wanted to drive somewhere, but it felt lonely.

My grandma came round. 'Did you pass?'

'Yes I did.'

'Good. You can take me to the library.'

PART 2

AVVAY

Chapter 10

Off the Road

Tony was Jack Kerouac cool. He walked into the lecture room that first morning with a matchstick in his mouth, wearing jeans with a Paisley flare that he later told us he'd got his mum to sew in.

Tony was everyone's friend. He had a firm handshake, good eye contact, and he was a good listener who made everyone feel interesting. He could charm his way into any party. He was always late because he was always in demand somewhere else. The boys wanted to be like him. The girls just wanted him. But he would never commit to anyone or anything. You could never contact him. He never gave his phone number or address. 'Don't tie me down,' he would say.

It was well into the term before I discovered that the reason Tony didn't give his phone number was because he didn't have a phone. He didn't have an address either. Tony lived in his car.

My father had been right. A driving licence gave me the sort of freedom every teenager dreams of. I spent the summer behaving like Richard Dreyfuss in *American Graffiti*, cruising around Bournemouth and Poole with a car full of friends, meeting up in the new multi-storey at the Arndale Centre – the only car park to be seen in that summer. I had no idea what I wanted to do.

'Get a job with British Leyland,' said Mr Besant over the fence.

Lots of people said that to me. They'd said it to my brother as well before he left home. The motor industry, so buoyant in the fifties and early sixties, had grown complacent and had been hit hard by the streamlined production techniques of Germany and Japan. The merger of the two British giants, BMC and Leyland Motors – who between them had already bought up most of the smaller marques – was going to re-establish our reputation. There was great excitement in 1971 when British Leyland announced that its first new car was to be launched.

The media pumped it up. Everyone wanted a glimpse of the saviour of British motoring. They whipped off the covers with great fanfare, and there it was: the Morris Marina.

No new car ever caught the public imagination less. They tried their best to make it look appealing; there was a TV commercial with a line of them on a beach at sunset. But no matter which angle they filmed the car from, it still looked like something the tide had washed up.

Car adverts like that never made me want to buy the car. But they did inspire me to want to work in advertising. I signed up for a two-year course in a college in north London. My parents stood outside the house as I packed the car.

'Have you checked the oil?' said my father.

'Yes.'

'Brake fluid?'

'Yes.'

'I'll just take the tyre pressures.'

I'd already checked the tyre pressures, but I let him get out his little pocket gauge, the same one he'd had all these years.

'I reckon it's about 129 miles,' he said.

'Right.'

'Write down the mileage now and when you get there, and you'll know exactly.'

I drove off. In the rear-view mirror I could see them waving, my father with his arm round my mother, comforting her as she watched her boy leave home.

By October they'd converted my bedroom into an office.

I was lucky to be a student and have a car, I knew that. But I certainly wasn't alone. That first day at college a number of us had keys on our desks with our cigarettes. Austin A40s were popular, Ford Anglias and old Cortinas. Tony had a Triumph Herald estate which was filled like a lost property office. It contained clothing and books, pots and pans, stacks of newspapers, a little stove, a set of cricket stumps. There was a pile of firewood and a bucket; cans of beans, a lot of rope, a guitar, an unloved pot plant. The vehicle was coloured two-tone black and lilac, but this was no showroom paint job; he'd done it himself, with a brush, so that the bodywork had the texture of an oil painting.

The thing that really defined Tony's Herald, though, was the sound system. At the start of the seventies it was by no means standard to have so much as a radio in a car, let alone a means of playing customized music. But Tony had his own setup, adapted from a home stereo to fit right around the car. There were speakers in all corners, wires looping everywhere. A cassette player was wedged between the seats, and tapes were lined up on little shelves secured to the roof.

He'd recorded every album worth listening to and lots that weren't, and he was a pioneer of the personalized tape. 'Best driving song ever?' said Tony as we piled in and headed off to nowhere in particular.

'"All Right Now" by Free.'

'Beatles, "Back In The USSR".'

'Led Zep, "Whole Lotta Love".'

'You're all wrong,' said Tony and he put on Steppenwolf. 'Born to be wiiiiild,' we sang, and cruised round the North Circular with the windows open and the volume up to max, playing drums on the dashboard and backs of seats, just driving for the fun of it.

When we first arrived at the college there was a rush to find accommodation. Most people found digs or got together and rented a flat and quickly settled in. Tony said he'd found digs too, but his car never got any less empty. He always had to throw things into the back to fit you in, or you sat with a box of tapes on your lap. No one minded; everyone wanted to travel with Tony.

'Get in, I'll give you a ride,' was his favourite line.

'Where are you going?'

'Wherever you want to go.'

Some evenings we'd head on up the M1, to the

motorway services at Scratchwood just a few miles north. We'd decided it was the cool place to be late at night. Bands would call in on their way back from gigs. They were noisy and badly behaved. The staff moaned: 'These new bands think they're special. We had Vince Hill in here last year. His table manners were impeccable.'

Cars were cheap to buy. Insurance was cheap. Petrol was cheap. Parts were cheap, or they were if you got them Tony's way.

'You've bust your back light,' he said to me one day.

I'd reversed into a post and smashed it. I'd taped it up, but it needed replacing.

'Jump in,' he said.

We drove out through east London with Frank Zappa playing. 'Top ten songs about London?'

'Kinks, "Waterloo Sunset".'

'Small Faces, "Itchycoo Park".'

'Bert Jansch, "Soho".'

Eventually we pulled into a wasteland where there was a graveyard of vehicles, piles of crashed cars balanced precariously on top of each other. I'd never seen anything like it, but Tony was an old hand. He nodded to the guys on the gate and we wandered round the creaking stacks.

Every model of car you'd ever seen on the road was there, each of them a corpse destined for the crusher at the other end of the yard. We quickly found a Morris 1000 – there were plenty to choose from – and I unscrewed the back reflector. Once you got started it was hard to stop. I found another Morris the same shade of blue as mine and removed the door panel and some carpet. The chrome rims round my headlights were rusting so I located a replacement set of those too.

Tony spied a Triumph Herald three cars high. He clambered up from bonnet to bonnet and climbed inside. I waited below, watching the pile wobble as he worked. Eventually he lowered a front seat down to me.

We could have spent the afternoon unscrewing bits and pieces, but then in one Herald Tony found blood stains on the steering wheel and that made us call it a day.

We took our haul to the man on the gate. 'What you got?' he said.

'Back light.'

'50p.'

'Headlight rims.'

'50p.'

How much is this seat?' asked Tony.

'50p.'

I never went to a garage for a spare part again.

'Have a look at this,' said Tony one day and showed me a picture of the Gravelly Hill Interchange on the M6 just out of Birmingham. It was such a knot of converging motorways, of flyovers and underpasses, that a local journalist had dubbed it Spaghetti Junction.

'We need to visit,' said Tony.

'I hate spaghetti,' I said. My experience had been of the tinned stuff, or alphabet spaghetti smothered in sweet sauce.

'Two birds with one stone,' said Tony.

That weekend four of us piled into the Herald and bombed up the M1. 'Top ten songs about spaghetti?' said Tony.

No one could think of one, until Tony slipped in a cassette and the music from *The Good, the Bad and the Ugly* began. He played that until we passed under a bridge with the graffiti *Clapton is God*, and the rest of the journey was dedicated to Eric Clapton and Cream.

Spaghetti Junction was difficult to grasp fully. Barbara Castle had called these motorway giants 'the cathedrals of the modern world', but it was such a tangle of tarmac it made little sense. 'Looks like a giant Scalextric,' I said.

'It looks like a bowline hitch,' said Tony.

There was an impressive ugliness at work here, but to appreciate it properly you really needed to be underneath it on the canal that weaved through all the concrete, or be one of the raptors hovering overhead.

'You wait,' said Tony. 'In 20 years' time it'll be a listed building.'

We had come to accept motorways as part of the landscape. They were familiar territory now, and we knew how they operated. The large blue signs were no longer so overwhelming, the service stations less formal. When we stopped at one on the way back there was no concern about how to behave. There was even a picnic site for Tony to get his stove out and cook up some spaghetti. A bit of egg and bacon and we dined alfresco on a carbonara as the cars flashed past us back to London.

Our lives revolved around cars and parties. That first term each of us in turn threw a bash at our flats. Tony was the only one not to, and this was what first made me think he'd never bothered to find anywhere to live.

''Bout time you threw a party eh, Tony?' I said, thinking he'd make some excuse, but he said, 'You're right. I'll have one tonight.'

'Where?'

'Meet me in the pub on the canal.'

We all gathered there, and stayed until closing time. 'Right, everyone back to my place,' said Tony. And he led us all to the corner of the car park by the lock gates where we found his Herald. He opened the back to reveal he'd cleared away all the mess and put out some sausage rolls.

'Tuck in,' he said, and cracked open a Party Seven with his tin opener.

A party in a car park felt odd to begin with, but then Tony's sound system kicked in. We sat on the lock gates singing along to his party tape, and soon we knew we were at the best party in town.

Afterwards, as his guests wandered off home, Tony said, 'Think I'll stay here the night,' and he quickly converted the back of the estate into a bed.

'Tony?' I said.

'What?'

'Do you live in your car?'

'Yeah.'

'Thought so.'

That wasn't so strange. Despite all the measures brought in to regulate the motorist – the 70mph speed limit, the breathalyser, the seat belt laws – cars still gave our generation a degree of freedom way beyond any other. The car underpinned youth culture. Tony's Herald was his beating heart, and he lived in it because it felt like home.

I can't honestly say, when Egyptian tanks rolled into the Sinai in October 1973, that I gave it much thought; nor when the Arab oil producers imposed an embargo shortly afterwards; nor even when rising oil prices prompted a three-day working week and the TV went off at 10.30. The only sleep I lost was due to the Three Day Week parties we threw. What do you expect from a bunch of self-centred students more interested in Pink Floyd than politics?

But when the price of petrol rose to the point that thieves started syphoning the stuff out of unguarded tanks, when Saudi Arabia's Sheik Yamani came on TV and said the era of cheap oil was gone, when petrol stations started to close, that was when we tuned in and took notice.

The nation panicked as usual. We assumed rationing was imminent. My father phoned and said, 'Time to stock up on bacon again.' The speed limit was even dropped from 70 to 50mph in an effort to conserve fuel.

But rationing never happened. Instead the price just rose steadily until no one could afford to drive, particularly students, particularly students like Tony. For a man who was defined by his car the oil crisis came as a big blow. 'It's not fair,' he kept saying, sadly, 'it's just not fair.'

I found him sitting in his car one day reading the newspaper: 'I mean, what have I got to do with the Arab–Israeli conflict?'

'Let's put some music on,' I said.

'Says here, this whole business stems back to the British inability to solve the Palestinian question at the end of World War I. Fifty years later the supply and price of oil is being controlled for political means and the result is I've got a car I can't drive.'

'Put some music on.'

'I can't. It runs down the battery.'

'Let's drive somewhere.'

And he looked at me helplessly.

I left my car outside my digs and started taking the bus. Some friends hung money boxes from their dashboard and tried to charge for a lift; others just sold their cars and were suddenly much better off. We met at the Wimpy bar instead of Scratchwood services. In 1972 Britain had produced almost two million cars – a record – and by 1973 no one could afford to run them.

Tony capitulated and found himself some accommodation. He emptied his car and took his sound system out. He wasn't the same man. He lost his faraway look; the matchstick chewing started to look silly. Now he had a room and a landlady who gave him an earful if he wasn't back at 5.30 for his evening meal. He tried to keep running his car. Once he offered me a lift home, but halfway he ran out of petrol. We pushed it back to his place.

It stood outside his house for the rest of the term. 'The trouble is,' he said, 'I can afford the petrol to go somewhere, but not to get back.' And that just about summed up the oil crisis for us.

We stopped seeing Tony. He stopped coming into lectures. I wondered if he'd dropped out. Then I saw him in the street one day, handing out leaflets.

'Have you seen what the motor car is doing to our green and pleasant land?' he said, and shoved a green piece of paper in my face that said 'Friends of the Earth'. 'Carbon monoxide fumes are polluting our air. Something has got to be done.'

'What's got to be done?'

'Catalytic converters.'

'What converters?'

'Read your bloody leaflet.'

In a fortnight Tony had gone from being a petrol-head to an environmentalist. From the coolest cat in college to a tree-hugger.

'And if you must drive,' he said, 'you should be driving Japanese cars.'

No, no! Japanese cars were tiny and ugly and probably made of fibreglass.

'Things are changing,' said Tony. 'The signs are everywhere. You know Lord Lucan?'

'Yes.'

'You know he did a runner from his flat leaving a dead nanny behind?'

'Yes.'

'Well what car do you think he drove off in?'

'I don't know.'

'A Datsun.'

Chapter 11

Driver Wanted

I never did apply for a job at British Leyland, which was just as well as the company went bankrupt in 1975.

They said it was the fault of poor industrial relations, on top of the oil crisis and the three-day week. But more likely it was the cars that were to blame, models like the Austin Allegro which actually achieved the impossible and made the Marina look stylish.

The government stepped in and effectively nationalized the company. The following year they employed a man named Michael Edwardes to run things. It was hard to take him seriously. He looked like Reg Varney from *On the Buses*.

My only connection with British Leyland was that I ended up driving one of their vans for a living. After 17 years of education this seemed unambitious even to me, but all I wanted to do was travel, to be on the move. Had finances allowed it I would have headed somewhere exotic, but they didn't, so I took an interest in the mundane, and the simplest way to do this was to sign on at the London Drivers' Agency. This was nothing more than a woman on the other end of the phone in Streatham who got you out of bed in the morning, and told you to get down to Wilkinson's Builders Merchants or somewhere similar, where you were handed the keys to a van and spent all day driving round delivering nuts and bolts. It was mindless, repetitive work, negotiating the London traffic all day. I loved it.

One morning I was sent to a company called Chaters in Islington. They wanted someone for the week. A transport manager named Jim who wore a brown coat like a grocer pointed me to a little van full of printing paper. He shuffled the list of printers I was to visit into order: 'You're going to City Road. That's good.'

'Why's that good?'

'The City Road Café.'

The City Road Café was better than good: salt beef sandwiches and pickled eggs, with a pint of tea and a bowl of bread and butter pudding. The rest of the day wasn't so successful. I got hopelessly lost round the back of the East End, and had to hurry to make the last delivery of the afternoon in Camden Passage, a narrow street of antique dealers and furniture importers off Islington Green. One of my wheels hit the kerb and jumped up. The steering wheel spun out of my hand and I hit a shop specializing in military history.

The owner ran out looking like he might stab me with an 18th-century bayonet. 'I've just had it all painted!' he screamed.

I tried to calm him down. 'It's just a scrape. Nothing broken. I'll fix it myself. I'll paint it.' I didn't want word getting back to base. This was a week's work at risk.

Back at the depot the first thing Jim said was, 'Heard you had a ding-dong up Camden Passage.'

'Yeah. Sorry.'

'Fill in an accident form. See you tomorrow?'

'See you tomorrow.'

The next day it didn't take me so long to have an accident. This time I went up the back of a car at some traffic lights. The driver got out. He was a big man, but he spoke in a very gentle manner. 'Just a scratch,' he said.

'Yeah, just a scratch.'

'And a dent.'

'A bit of a dent, yeah, you're right.'

There was traffic building up behind us, but he walked slowly round his car. 'And there's another scratch there, look.'

'Actually, I'm not sure I did that.'

'I'm pretty sure you did. And this dent.'

'That definitely wasn't me.'

He smiled. The traffic was honking now. He got an old envelope out of his pocket and wrote down all the details. 'I'd appreciate it if you signed this.'

He wanted me to sign full responsibility for the accident and all the damage. 'I don't think I can do that,' I said.

'Sign it,' he said, no longer the gentle giant, more a big man doing his best to control his aggression. I signed it.

When I got back that evening Jim didn't look happy. He marched towards me with his finger pointing. 'You... had another accident.'

'Yes. Sorry.'

'Don't ever, ever, ever, admit responsibility for anything. Ever.'

'Right.'

'Is that clear?'

'Yes.'

'See you tomorrow.'

'See you tomorrow.'

It went on like this for the whole week. I'd come in at the end of the day, and say, 'I had a bump on Stroud Green Road.'

'Good café on Stroud Green Road.'

'But I didn't accept responsibility.'

'You're learning.'

By Friday my van looked as though it had been driven into battle. I'd forgotten which scars were from which accident. But I'd survived the week and I was happy with that. When I dropped the keys off Jim took me to one side. 'How was it today?'

'Fine.'

'Nobody's phoned to say you hit them or anything.'

'No, I don't think I had an accident today.'

'Do you want the job full time?'

'Er... okay.'

'See you Monday morning. Got a nice new van for you.'

The new van was a truck really, a British Leyland Terrier. I nicknamed it Ivan. It wasn't new, but it was a lot newer than anything I should have been given. It was brown and butch, and as I climbed into the cab that first morning it felt very, very big. 'Am I allowed to drive this?' I asked Jim.

'It's only a three tonner.'

I set off up the Holloway Road. I towered above the London traffic. I thought: I could really do some damage in this vehicle.

Jim began to give me routes out of London. Soon I found myself in the world of the commercial driver: the transport cafés, the *Sun*, the roll-ups. The drivers all moaned about everything from road works to the emotional trauma of running over a hedgehog. I moaned along with them in solidarity, although the truth was I'd never enjoyed a job so much. I was being paid to have trips to Kent and the south coast. I even got paid for having lunch. 'Forgot to give you these last week,' Jim had said, and handed me a stash of Luncheon Vouchers.

Jim was a connoisseur of transport cafés. Some of the places he directed me to were legendary, but not always for their food. He told me to visit a café in Swindon, so I did, and it was horrible. 'I know it's horrible,' said Jim, 'but what you've got to realize is it's been horrible for twenty years.'

After a couple of weeks he said to me, 'Are you married?'

'No.'

'Want to do the overnighter to East Anglia?'

He was offering it to me because none of the other drivers wanted to spend the night away. Don, who used to do the run, said, 'The missus doesn't like me going away; she thinks I get up to no good.'

I'd never been to East Anglia before. In fact when I told people I was going there, 'I've never been to East Anglia' was what most of them said. I looked at the map. The towns had comedy names like Bungay and Beccles. I'd never heard of these places. I felt like a missionary taking printing paper into the unknown.

I took the M1 north to Northampton and then headed east into the fens. It was mid-winter and the grey land merged with the grey sky miles in the distance. The roads were flat and featureless; the towns huddled together, beaten by the weather.

In such a landscape the roadside cafés were like oases. One place near Downham Market made its own steak and kidney pudding, and they handed you a plateful as you walked in whether you wanted it or not. The drivers sat with their heads in steaming suet. There was something of the opium den about the place. When I finished my meal I turned to see a woman with red forearms standing over me holding out something mountainous and yellow. 'Crumble,' she said, and handed it to me as if it was Holy Communion, brought straight from the apple crumble mines of Thetford.

My route would take me along the north Norfolk coast to Fakenham and Cromer, then down to Great Yarmouth where the funfair had been put away for the winter and the beach was a bleak dog-walk. I had a radio and the heater on, and enough Luncheon Vouchers to feed a coach party. I felt as free as the oystercatchers wheeling over the marshes.

In those days few trucks had beds in the back, and so lorry drivers' boarding houses were common. Don had told me about a place to stay in Lowestoft, 'cheap and not very cheerful'. A woman in an apron opened the door when I knocked.

'What you carrying?'

'Printing paper.'

She nodded. Looked me over. Sniffed me, checked I wasn't covered in oil, then ushered me in. 'Room 6, top of the stairs. No shoes on the bed.'

Room 6 had four other drivers in it, all lying on their beds with their shoes off, all smoking and reading the *Sun*.

They nodded at me. I sat on the only vacant bed. 'What you carrying?' said one of them.

'Printing paper. You?'

'Dog food.'

'Plastics,' said another.

'Where's Don?' said another.

'He's not doing it any more.'

'His missus must have found out.' He put his paper down and said, 'You want a game of draughts?'

His name was Pat and I played draughts with him for two hours. He beat me 32 games to nothing. The thrashing was only ended by the landlady kicking open the door and shouting: 'It's ready!'

We all sat squashed together at a little table as the food was dished out. It was the kind of meal that reminded you that you were British. Lowestoft was a fishing port, but this meal looked inland: a lot of meat, a lot of gravy, a lot of pudding. The only way to tell the difference between the courses was by their colour.

'Anyone want seconds?' said the landlady. Not one of us wanted seconds but, equally, not one of us wanted to incur her wrath by saying so. Afterwards I felt like I'd eaten a great lump of Suffolk.

I hauled myself outside and walked round the harbour. In the tourist office window I learnt that Lowestoft is the most easterly point in Britain. So I walked to the end of the Ness and for five minutes I was the most easterly person in the country, until a couple came and stood nearby and I backed off. It didn't seem fair to hog the title.

When I got back to the boarding house all the drivers were in bed. I lay there in the glow of the street light listening to them all snore, dreaming of dog food and plastics. When I woke at 7.30 they had all gone. I went downstairs for breakfast and the landlady said to me, 'What time do you call this? Breakfast finished half an hour ago.'

'Oh, what a shame.'

My parents took the news that I was driving a van in different ways. 'You're putting on weight,' said my mother.

'I know what you're doing,' said my father. 'I know your ploy.'

'What ploy?'

'Starting out on the shop floor. Very wise.'

I'd already let slip that I had plans to be a writer. My mother said, 'Two words of advice: Harold and Robbins.'

My father's reaction was more muted. This wasn't because he was disappointed, but because he couldn't envisage a career path. But now that I had a job driving for a printing paper company, he saw a plan: writers wrote books, and books were made from paper. I was simply gaining experience in the print room. Just as it would have made sense to get a job at Dulux had I wanted to be a painter.

He had a surprise for me as well. There was a new, powder blue Ford Capri standing in the drive. 'A black vinyl top,' he said, and lovingly stroked the roof.

Vinyl was what LPs and wallpaper were made out of. What was it doing on a car roof?

'It's got a proper roof underneath,' he said.

'What possessed you?'

'Thought I'd put a bit of fun back into motoring.'

In fact, he had been possessed by television. For years he'd scoffed when we suggested he buy a Volvo like Simon Templar in *The Saint*, or a Lotus like Patrick McGoohan in *The Prisoner*. 'I'm not really a Lotus type of chap.'

But the marketing departments of motor manufacturers had become smarter over the years. If the hero of a TV show drove one of your company's cars, while his nemesis drove one made by your competitor, it was a huge publicity coup, particularly if your car came out of a car chase still standing and your competitor's rolled a couple of times and got towed away. It was the kind of advertising money couldn't buy.

My father was a hard nut to crack, but this sort of product placement eventually worked on him thanks to his favourite TV series, *Minder*. I would have thought he identified with George Cole's Arthur Daley and his Jaguar XJ6. But no, it was Dennis Waterman's Terry McCann and his Ford Capri that seduced him.

'It's my fault,' said my mother. 'I bought him that digital watch at Christmas and he's not been the same since.'

He wore an open shirt at the wheel now instead of a cravat. He smoked cigarettes instead of a pipe, and he sat there with the long, slim bonnet in front of him, trying to look as though he still had a tiger in his tank.

'It's only got two doors,' I said. 'You vowed you'd never have a car with two doors.'

'A man has to change with the times, you know.'

'How does Grandma get in?'

'Sore point.'

The point was sore because she couldn't get in. She took a taxi to the library now.

'She's lost patience with cars,' said my mother. 'Ever

since the Queen started driving round in a Range Rover.'

'Have I told you, it's got a vinyl roof?' said my father.

'Yes you have. Can I take it for a spin?'

He paled. A man might have to change with the times, but there was no way he was ever going to let any of his children near his car.

I got to know East Anglia so well I could have driven around it without a map, which was useful because there was rarely anyone to ask for directions if I got lost. Driving across the fens was like driving through space. If I did see someone walking along the road I'd always stop and ask if they were all right or wanted a lift. In the middle of March the landscape didn't seem capable of ever bursting into spring. It looked as though it had been winter for centuries.

I began to feel comfortable as a van driver. I put a Bruce Springsteen poster up in the cab. I became adept at rolling my own. I knew the names of the women who worked in the transport cafés. Thanks to my nights in Lowestoft I became a much better draughts player.

But I knew this job couldn't go on much longer. I was aware there was a whole world out there beyond Norwich. Also my mother was right – I was putting on far too much weight.

One night in Lowestoft a Norwegian driver turned up. You could tell he was foreign because he didn't take his boots off before he lay on the bed. He didn't have an apple crumble gut either. He wore a white T-shirt and a leather waistcoat that showed off his biceps and his tattoos. He talked us through them: 'This one of the mermaid I got in Rotterdam. This one of the tiger I got in Hamburg. And this one of the sardine I got in Helsinki.'

The English drivers muttered. 'Looks more like a herring,' said Pat, who had worked on the boats.

The door crashed open and the landlady yelled, 'It's ready!'

The others padded down the stairs. But the Norwegian laughed. He wasn't going to eat in a boarding house. He told me to come with him into town to find somewhere else. 'You English,' he laughed. 'You drive on the left and your food tastes like shit.'

He marched me into a Greek taverna. He ordered Retsina and a huge amount to eat. 'I mean, what sort of people invent bread and butter pudding?'

'It can vary, I agree.'

'And your stupid full English breakfasts.'

'Steady on.'

'You need to drive in Germany or Italy.'

He told me stories of the wonderful truck stops in Bavaria where they had whole hogs roasting on a spit; or in Tuscany where they rolled their own pasta. 'Fresh ravioli with pecorino and wild mushrooms.'

'Have you ever tried toad in the hole?' I said.

'I once had a meal in Poland where they gave me lung soup. Delicious. Illegal but delicious.'

The food arrived and he said thank you in Greek to the waiter.

Afterwards we wandered down to the water. Fishing boats were getting ready to go out for the night. 'Where are you going next?' I asked.

'Madrid,' he said, and spat.

I knew it was time to make a move. I was tempted to just drive the Terrier onto a boat down the road at Harwich and head off through Europe. No one at the depot would know I was gone until Monday.

There didn't seem to be any other way of getting out. But then the winter of '76 finally turned into the summer of '76 and with it came the perfect escape route.

Chapter 12

The Hitchhiker's Guide to Norfolk

It was the age of the hitchhiker. Throughout the sixties and seventies no lay-by or motorway on-ramp was complete without a hitcher standing there. Some were clutching trade plates and wanting a lift home after delivering a car; some were students travelling home; one or two were serial killers, or so the story went. Hitchhikers were part of roadside furniture. Some drivers picked them up, some didn't.

My father never picked them up. 'Why not?' I asked.

'I'm only going down the road. Hitchhikers hate you picking them up and dropping them a few hundred yards away.'

But he never picked them up when he was going on a long journey either. Once on the way to London we passed a couple of teenagers with long hair and tie-dye shirts. 'Let's pick them up,' I said.

'There's nowhere to stop.' That old excuse.

'They're standing right by a lay-by.'

'Don't worry, someone will pick them up.'

He was right of course: hitchhikers did get picked up, and anyway it would have been awful to have had them in our car. My father would have spent the whole journey to London trying to convince two hippies why they should start paying into a pension scheme early.

When I became a van driver I was faced with the same dilemma: to pick up or not to pick up. The company policy was predictable, but it just felt rude to leave people standing there when I was going a distance, and once I'd started I found I couldn't stop.

In that glorious summer of '76 hitchhiking peaked. They were on every motorway slip-road, every roundabout. At the start of the M1 at Staples Corner there had always been one or two, even through the winter, but as the summer settled in the numbers grew. One morning there was a line of them waiting, sitting on their bags on the slip-road, soaking up the sun. I stopped at the first one: 'Where you going?'

'Scotland.'

'Jump in.'

Then on to the next, a couple: 'Where you going?'

'York.'

'Jump in.'

When the cab was full I opened the back and the rest climbed up and sat on the printing paper. I must have had ten hitchhikers on board, and now we were speeding up the motorway.

They came from all over the world. Lots of North Americans and Australians, many from Scandinavia. With the windows open and the Bedfordshire countryside looking as golden as it ever would, England was part of the global tour. I imagined I was driving the Magic Bus, but instead of going to Kathmandu we were heading for Northampton.

One couple from New Zealand had come all the way overland. They looked dusty and weary and very thin. I asked them what had been the best place they'd visited. They said they had really enjoyed Brighton.

Normally I dropped the hitchers as I left the motorway or at a nearby services, but one week an American lad asked where I was heading. When I told him East Anglia he said he'd like to stick with me. 'Don't you want to go to York and places, like everyone else?'

'My ancestors come from East Anglia.'

He stayed with me for the two days, and as we motored along the coast and then down to the Broads, we both wondered how his family could ever have left. That summer Norfolk was as dry as everywhere else, but looked so sun-kissed. I noticed windmills for the first time and the coastline was brimming with boats. Ken was one of those Americans who knew more about England than most Englishmen. He had a rucksack full of maps and guides. 'What's that tower in the distance?'

'I don't know.' I'd seen it every Thursday since January and often wondered what it was, but never bothered to find out.

It was Ely Cathedral, sitting out on the fens like some grounded galleon. You could see it for miles around.

We made a detour. I drove across the raised roads with the cathedral looming larger and larger; the little town that had sprung up around it looked Lilliputian in its shadow. I parked next to an ice-cream van and we went inside.

It was beautifully cool and quiet after the dust and rumble of the truck. Ken strolled with his head up and mouth open, gazing up at the marble columns. He bought another guide: 'Shit, this place is 537 feet long.'

'So where in East Anglia are your family from?'

'I don't know. I didn't think to ask. They left in 18-something.'

The history lesson continued on the road to King's Lynn and past Sutton Bridge. 'Hey, slow down,' said Ken. 'This is where King John lost the crown jewels.'

'You're kidding.'

'That's what it says here.'

Every schoolboy knew the story of King John losing his baggage train somewhere in the Wash, but I'd no idea I'd been driving over the very spot all winter. We walked down to the river and took a cursory look round, hoping we might get lucky and see a crown sticking out of the mud. 'Says his wagons sunk into the swampy marsh,' said Ken.

In every direction there was swampy marsh. 'Any other clues?' I said.

'Says the land has been eroded and the place where the baggage train sunk is probably out at sea.'

We walked to the other side of the swing bridge, towards the sea. Still no sign of any jewels.

'I guess you've got to use your imagination,' said Ken. And we both stood there and watched the gulls and tried to use our imagination for a bit.

From the coast we drove down through the Broads. The evening was balmy and there was water lapping everywhere. With the hot weather I no longer stayed in the boarding house. I just parked up somewhere out of the way, then slept on the paper in the back of the van, and saved the accommodation money. We found a field of stubble to hide in and walked off to a pub.

'Did you know that these aren't rivers at all?' said Ken, eyes in his book.

'What are they?'

'They're peat bogs. "It was only in the 1960s that it was discovered that the channels are artificial features, the effect of flooding on medieval peat excavations."'

'Yeah, yeah... I knew that.'

I was getting tired of being lectured on my own country by an American. There was a shelf full of games in the pub. 'Do you want a game of draughts, Ken?'

'Checkers? I've haven't played checkers for years.'

'You never forget.'

We played 20 games and, using Pat's gambits, I thrashed Ken each time.

We went back to the field and crawled into sleeping bags. But then in the middle of the night Ken got up.

'What's happening?'

'It's three o'clock,' he said, and jumped down from the van.

'Where are you going?'

'I need to call home.'

He walked back to the phone box by the pub. When he returned he said, 'Do you know somewhere called Saxmundham?'

'We're going there tomorrow.'

'That's where my family come from.'

Phew, What a Scorcher! said the *Sun* the next day, just as it had said most days that summer, adding: *Tarmac Melts as Britain Swelters.* It was true, the tarmac was melting. You could peel it off the side of the roads if you felt so inclined.

We drove to Great Yarmouth first thing. The funfairs were open, the sands packed by ten o'clock. We delivered to a printer and the staff were all working in shorts. Their shift had started at five o'clock that morning so that they could finish at lunchtime and have the afternoon on the beach. We did another drop in Beccles and then Southwold, and by lunchtime we were driving into Saxmundham.

Ken was feeling very nervous.

'What's the matter?'

'There might be people here who look like me.'

He checked all the shop fronts to see if any bore the name Woodman, but none did. When we made our delivery he asked if there were any people called Woodman in town. No one knew of any.

Ken looked in the phone book. No Woodman.

He tried to hide his disappointment. We bought some pork pies and went into the churchyard. I sat down on a bench in the sun, and as Ken looked round the graves, I realized I'd learned more about East Anglia in the past two days than I had in the whole of the previous six months.

Ken yelled from the other side of the church. I found him rubbing a headstone, trying to make the lettering more clear. 'Look, Woodman.'

The grave was two hundred years old but that didn't bother him. There was a chance this person was his great-great-great-something. He took a picture. He got me to take a picture of him standing next to the stone. Then he took a picture of me standing next to the gravestone. I smiled for the camera, but I was smiling because I knew that this little scene was only happening because Ken had been standing with his thumb out at Staples Corner. Hitchhiking opened up limitless possibilities. It was the solution to all I wanted to do.

Chaters announced they were moving out of London to Surrey. 'There's a job for you if you want to move with us,' said Jim. I declined; all the drivers did.

The only person disappointed was my father. 'You were on the ladder there. It was time to make your play for the sales office.'

'I don't think so.'

'No matter. The good news is I've spoken to a contact who knows someone who is a publisher. He's going to give you an interview.'

Having gained experience in the transport department of the writing business, now he thought it would be sensible to learn about the editorial process.

'Where's the interview?'

'Edinburgh.'

I said okay, simply because I wanted to go to Edinburgh. I was going to buy a car with the money I'd saved from working all summer, but first I wanted to try my luck at something else.

I took a bus to Staples Corner and stuck out my thumb. There were no other hitchhikers, but that may have been because it was pouring with rain. The heatwave had got so bad the government had appointed a Minister for Drought, and, of course, within a couple of days the country was flooded and he became Minister of Floods.

I stood there with my hood up, water running down

my nose. Hitchhiking looked more fun than this from the driving seat. I eyeballed all the van drivers; I was owed a lift. Eventually a car pulled in. 'I'm going to Luton,' he said.

He was an orthopaedic mattress salesman and spent the whole trip trying to sell me a bed. I declined his offer. But this made him go quiet, so I said, 'Actually, maybe I could do with a new bed,' which got him going again. I was appalled at the way I was willing to sell myself for a ride, but he looked like he would have taken me all the way to Scotland if he thought he could make a sale.

Two headbangers picked me up next, on their way to a heavy metal concert. They played Black Sabbath all the way to Leicester. 'You like Sabbath?' one of them asked.

'Love 'em,' I said, which was all I could say, really.

'We'll drop you off at the service station,' they said. 'It's a great place to hitch.'

I spent two hours trying to get out of the service station. A sign was what I needed, so I found some cardboard and wrote *Edinburgh* out in big letters. Or they started big, but got smaller and smaller as they reached the end, until the letters G and H were crawling vertically up the side.

A car stopped; the driver peered at the sign, as if he couldn't recognize anywhere in Britain spelt like that. I opened the door. 'I'm only going to Peebles,' he said.

'Where's that?'

'About ten miles outside Edinburgh.'

For the next six hours I learnt all about his job as a PE teacher; how he'd just been to Berkhamsted to help his aged mother move house; how he had been an aspiring rugby player until a knee injury made him retire. He told me about Edinburgh and what it was like to live there, and where I should look for a flat if I got the job. He told me about his two children and how one was hitchhiking across America, which was why he picked me up. 'Where does he stay?' I asked.

'He says people who give him lifts take him home and put him up.'

'Strangers?'

'Strangers.'

We pulled into a services at the border and he bought me a meal. 'I'm after good karma,' he said.

I got to Edinburgh and stayed the night in a hostel. The interview went all right, but the hitchhike home was more important. One driver offered me a job fruit picking on his farm; another had a couch in the back of his van and asked me to help him move it into his house.

Hitchhiking just seemed like a win-win situation. The hitcher got a lift and often met someone with local information, and the driver got company, which was presumably why he had stopped, plus he felt he was doing someone a good turn. It was the means of travel I had been looking for. There were one or two weirdos, and some drivers who drove so dangerously I just wanted to get out, but generally here was an activity that depended on trust and kindness, an arrangement made possible by the motor car. It brought out the best in people.

I didn't get the job in Edinburgh. I didn't buy a car. Inspired by all the people I had picked up over the summer, and by the story of the young man who was being looked after by complete strangers in America, I bought a Freddie Laker ticket to New York and spent the next year hitchhiking coast to coast.

Chapter 13

Stop Thief

I went to fill up my mother's car at Mr Goodall's garage. He stepped out of his little kiosk and slipped the pump nozzle into the tank. Self-service stations were nationwide now, but Mr Goodall still eschewed them for the personal touch.

'That's two star,' I said.

'That's right.'

'I thought my father had four.'

'He puts four star in his car, two star in your mother's.'

My father claimed he had embraced equality of women, but his true politics always surfaced when it came to cars.

'Have they told you I'm retiring?' said Mr Goodall.

'Yes. I'm sorry to hear that.'

'It's those Smurfs that have pushed me over the edge.'

He was referring to the extended Smurf family, the troll-like figures given away at National petrol stations. They were the latest free gifts in the promotional wars between fuel companies that saw them try to lure the customer with coffee mugs, wine glasses, and endless tea towels and commemorative coins.

Mr Goodall filled the tank up and handed me a strip of Green Shield Stamps, five yards long.

'What's all this?'

'Quadruple stamps. That's all I've got to battle the Smurfs with. I mean be honest, what would you rather have: a roll of stamps or a Smurf?' He spoke as if he wanted to strangle the entire Smurf family in their sleep.

No one really believed the gifts were free of course. They just meant higher petrol prices. But as usual the oil companies knew best: 'Consumers say they would rather have cheap petrol and no free gifts, but we don't think that's true.'

The lesser-known brands were disappearing. Names like Fina, Butler and Zip had all but gone, swallowed by the giants Total, Texaco, BP and Shell, which owned the fuel stations and had shops and car washes on site. Mr Goodall had done his best to compete. He was always open. There was a bell on the wall you could ring in the middle of the night and he'd come out and give you petrol in his pyjamas. But he couldn't survive any more.

'So I'm closing down. I'm having a half-price sale.'

I looked in his shop display. There was a tin of polish that had been there since 1958 and not much else. But then I noticed a card in the window advertising a Ford Escort for £500.

'Very good runner,' said Mr Goodall. 'Ten years old and only 100,000 on the clock. £500.'

'I thought everything was half-price.'

'Very funny. I can probably get him down to £480.'

I needed a car. I was living in London, working as a gardener and cycling everywhere. This was becoming impractical though. As business picked up I needed to carry tools around with me. Also, cycling in London in the seventies was a minority activity as dangerous as swimming with sharks. The environmentalist movement was growing, but supporters were still looked upon as sandal-wearing dreamers, and as far as the average motorist was concerned cyclists were just a nuisance. I had to assume every car was going to cut me up, every car door open in front of me, every bus flatten me. I needed a car for work but also for my own protection.

I paid Mr Goodall the £480 for the Escort. 'It's a deal,' he said, then handed me the keys and logbook, and threw a whole roll of Green Shield Stamps on the back seat.

I drove it back to London and parked it outside my flat. It was stolen that night.

The trouble with Ford Escorts, I soon learned, wasn't that they were underpowered or liable to rust; it was that they kept getting nicked. They were so nondescript that you wouldn't notice one if it was parked in your living room, making them the perfect car for the opportunist criminal.

Or so the policeman told me the following morning when I went down to Acton Police Station. I'd been phoned and told my car had been used in a crime and abandoned.

'So who stole it?'

'No idea. It was just left on the street.'

'Aren't you going to catch them?'

He looked at me as if I was making a joke. 'It's a Ford Escort.'

'So?'

'So you'll have to get used to it.'

The car wasn't damaged. The only things stolen were my spade and rake. I bought a locking device. But three nights later it was stolen again. This time it was abandoned in Harlesden. I cycled up to the police station to collect it. 'What happened?' I asked.

'It was consigned in a crime.'

'What crime?'

'Off-licence robbery on the Harrow Road.'

Once again no damage done. There were no bullet holes along the side or anything. Just the smashed remains of the new lock.

I didn't know what to do next. The crooks knew where it was parked now. Word had gone round that there was a pale blue Escort on my street. They could at least have abandoned it back outside my flat so I could use it for work the next morning.

I bought a very large padlock and a huge chain and chained the steering wheel to the seat. Then parked it three streets away. It made no difference. It was stolen within a couple of nights. It was as if it had a ring-pull top. This time I went to a police station in Putney.

The officer said, 'Ah yes, the Escort. It was...'

'... consigned in a crime. I know.'

'It's parked on the street round the side of the station.'

I walked the length of the street, but couldn't find it. The officer came out to help, but he couldn't find it either. 'I parked it right here,' he said.

We looked at each other for a moment. We both knew what had happened: someone had stolen it from outside the police station. As we stood there it was probably being used in a warehouse robbery down at Heathrow.

The summer came and there was a lull. The London crooks must have all gone on holiday and I was able to use the car instead of them.

The most fun you could have with a vehicle in London was driving through the West End at night, particularly if you came in on the Westway. This elevated motorway from Shepherd's Bush to the Euston Road had been open for ten years, but it was still a novelty and offered a futuristic ride into town as it carried you above the streets and houses, the red rear lights of the traffic ahead curving away into the night, speeding into the heart of the city.

Park Lane was also a thrill at night, even in a cheap Escort, and navigating Hyde Park Corner was like a ride at the dodgems. Then down past Buckingham Palace to the river, where the lights of the Embankment looped away downstream, until a crossing over Waterloo or Blackfriars Bridge, the inky water alight with reflections; ending up in a multi-storey at the South Bank (where the car was invariably nicked).

Driving to work during the day, though, was more of a challenge. Each morning I had to commute up to the rarefied gardens of Hampstead and Highgate, and I had hoped driving rather than cycling would save me time. But it rarely did. On a bike I could weave through traffic, take shortcuts along the canal tow path and across Hampstead Heath. In a car I just sat in a queue and fumed.

Parking in London was becoming a trial as well, as authorities used ever more aggressive measures. Traffic wardens had been a reliable source of revenue for years, but they didn't clear the streets of vehicles that blocked the highway. When clearways came in this was a problem that could only be solved with brute force, as I discovered when I went to visit my old friend Tony.

Tony had got into motorbikes. 'You should dump your car,' he said. 'If we all rode bicycles and motorbikes you'd solve London's traffic problems overnight.'

Like his car, Tony's bike always needed work doing to it. His living-room floor was covered in newspaper and there were engine bits everywhere.

'Do you know what you're doing?' I said.

'Sure. You take it apart, then you put it back together, and then you throw away the bits left over.'

We had too many beers and I stayed the night. In the morning when I went out to my car it was gone.

'My car's been nicked again,' I said as Tony handed me a mug of tea with an oily thumb print on it.

'That's an urban clearway out there.'

'So?'

'Anything in the way gets towed.'

I phoned the police. My car had indeed been towed away. I went down to the pound and there was a queue of hungover people waiting, all having to hand over £50 to get their car returned. At least when crooks took it they didn't want money to give it back.

In a city with such congestion, and where there was good and cheap public transport, a car began to seem like a liability, and when the Escort developed engine problems I wondered whether it was all really worth it. Tony had a look and said we needed to 'take the head off and grind down the valves'. We spent a weekend on it. Now my living-room floor was littered with engine bits, a cylinder head in the fireplace. On the Saturday we took it apart and did the work. On the Sunday we were going to put it back together again, but when Tony came round, he said, 'Where's the car gone?'

'It's outside.'

'No it's not.'

I thought he was joking. How could the car have been stolen with its cylinder head missing? But it was no joke. I was about to phone the police when, as usual, they phoned me. The car was a few hundred yards away, they said.

The inside had been wrecked: a Stanley knife taken to the seats; wires pulled out from under the dash. A bottle of anti-freeze had been poured over the outside, the doors kicked in, lights smashed. It was violent. We could only imagine that someone had tried to steal it, couldn't start it, so had pushed it down the road in an effort to bump it. When that failed they'd got angry.

We pushed it home and Tony helped me spend the rest of the week trying to make it roadworthy. It was never the same though, and looked as beat up as a stock car. The smart little runner I had bought from Mr Goodall had, within six months, become a jalopy.

And then the starter motor started playing up. 'You have to hit it with a hammer,' said Tony.

That was the kind of mechanics I could understand.

'Seriously,' he said. 'It frees it up.'

He tapped the starter motor with a hammer and it worked.

One night shortly afterwards I had a dream. I was trying to start the car and it was being reluctant as usual. 'You need to hit it,' I said. 'Hit it with a hammer.' Then I woke up. But the starter motor was still groaning.

I hurried to the window. The Escort had two figures in it.

I had no clothes on. I was dialling 999 and trying to pull on trousers at the same time. What was I thinking? Was I really going to go out there and tackle two villains? 'There's someone stealing my car,' I whispered to the officer.

'Name...?'

'I'm going down now to deal with them.'

'You stay where you are!'

'Okay, officer. Whatever you say.'

The car started and I watched them drive off.

But within five minutes the police had caught them. Two officers picked me up and took me down to the station where I gave a statement. 'I was about to go out there, but the officer said to stay where I was.' As I was leaving, I passed an interview room and there was one of the thieves being questioned. I looked at him through the glass panel in the door and he turned and looked back at me. I held his stare for a moment and his look said one thing: revenge.

Forensics kept the car for a day or two, but then I got it back and used it for work as normal. The summer holidays were over and the queues were worse than ever. It took me half an hour to get through Swiss Cottage one morning. I got angry and tried to push in and almost squashed a cyclist. He gave me a mouthful and I agreed with every word he said. I was beginning to realize where my heart lay.

Things came to a head at the end of the week. The front wheel of the car had been making a strange noise all morning. I had a look, but there didn't seem anything wrong so I kept going. I was on Westbourne Grove when the car suddenly lurched and sort of collapsed. My eye was caught by the surreal sight of my front wheel rolling freely down the road.

It was the embarrassment of it all that I'll never forget. The way people stopped and looked. The way the waiters in a curry house came out and stood on the pavement, watching me scratch my head.

A police car turned up and made me get a breakdown truck to tow it home. The mechanic had a look at it. 'Your wheel nuts have come loose somehow,' he said. 'You mucked about with them recently?'

'No.'

'Well someone has.'

I felt a shiver. The guys who stole the car the previous week had come back and had their revenge. There was no other explanation. 'Tell the police,' said my father. But I'd had enough of the police, and they had had enough of me.

The Escort wasn't worth repairing. I went back to riding my bike and decided only to garden for people who had their own tools.

I didn't have the heart to tell Mr Goodall. When I went home and saw him in town he asked after the car and I said it was fine: 'You were right, a good little runner.'

His garage had gone. The premises had become a delicatessen. He said he'd never been in there because it would make him feel sad, and they only sold foreign stuff anyway.

'The end of an era,' said my father, a row of Smurfs on the sideboard behind him.

He was right. Within a year Mr Goodall was dead.

Chapter 14

The Road
to Nowhere

With the rail network decimated, for many years Britain's roads groaned under the burden of extra freight. By the mid-eighties pollution and the impact of traffic on the environment had become so great it was clear transport policy needed to be radically reformed. The government agreed with this. So did the British Road Federation. Together they came up with a familiar solution: build more roads.

Margaret Thatcher loved roads. All politicians did. Roads gave people freedom and independence to do business. Sierra Man – the forerunner of Mondeo Man – came of age in the eighties, as he charged round Middle England on the motorway network, driving the free market economy that made the Thatcher government sleep so well at night.

Thatcher loved cars too. The day in 1984 when Nissan started production in Sunderland was the day Britain stopped being 'the sick man of Europe'. My father was a great fan of Margaret Thatcher, and enjoyed telling my mother she looked like her. There was a certain amount of truth in this, and at times, when she wore a blue dress and had just had her hair done, it was difficult not to talk politics with her. When it was announced in the local paper that there was to be extension of the M27 I looked her in the eye and said, 'You don't care about the environment one jot, do you?'

'Don't talk to the PM like that,' said my father. 'Besides, you can't stand in the way of progress.'

Actually, you *could* stand in the way of progress, as he proved when he sided with the protesters when the same newspaper announced that a bypass was to be built in the field next to his house.

'I'm not standing for it,' he said. 'What about the environment? They can't slice up the countryside willy-nilly just for a bypass.'

'You've been saying there should be a bypass for years.'

'There are far better places for a bypass.'

It was the cry of the Nimby nationwide. My father tried to galvanize the neighbours and form a protest group. Not one of them joined. They had all just had a letter from the council advising them that home owners in the immediate vicinity of the new road would receive compensation. This changed everything. Rather than seeing the bypass as an assault on the defenceless landscape and local community, residents began to see it as a chance to make money.

As a surveyor by profession my father imagined he had insider knowledge. 'No one knows the vagaries of the property market like I do,' he sniggered. 'I'll have them for every penny.' When the council made an offer, he wrote back saying it was risible and he wouldn't accept it. They wrote back saying he could take it or leave it, the bypass was going to be built whatever. He wrote back saying he'd take it.

He accepted defeat. He was retired and didn't want any more stress. As work started on the bypass he tried to ignore it. When that became impossible he planted leylandii trees all around the house and cut himself off from the rest of the world.

Bypasses had this kind of bipolar effect. One group would campaign to have them built, while another would lie down in front of the bulldozers. We wanted to have good roads, but we wanted to have them running through other people's gardens, not our own.

The eighties were the golden years of the bypass, and the longest, most emotionally exhausting bypass of them all was being built round the town I lived in: London. It was 1986, and after ten years of construction work, the last section of the M25 was about to open. It would soon be possible to drive round the capital in a circle forever.

I was driving a borrowed VW Beetle at the time. It was a lucky car. I left the handbrake off once as I parked it outside a shop. When I came back it was gone. Not another theft, I sighed. But a man cutting his hedge said, 'Is that your car?' He was pointing to the VW nestling against the kerb at the bottom of the cul-de-sac. It had navigated the whole street, through two rows of parked cars, entirely on its own.

'Yes, I think it is,' I said.

'You're a lucky bastard.'

I was trying to make a living travel writing, which meant I was away a lot, in Britain and abroad. The travelling was undeniably fun, but the writing was mostly short articles, and I wanted to do something more ambitious, a book perhaps. For that, though, I needed an original journey, and there just didn't seem to be any of those left.

Everywhere had been discovered, travelled through and written about. The most isolated points on earth had been reached on roller-skates. I spent a long time in the library trying to come up with a trip that no one else had done before. When I finally found one it was right on my doorstep.

The M25 was a brand new journey, a new habitat. It might not have had the same edge as a trek through the desert or the jungle, but it was an entirely original idea, a newly built route on fresh, warm tarmac. And no one could have done it yet because it wouldn't exist for another fortnight when Margaret Thatcher officially opened it.

I went back to the library and studied maps, researching places like South Mimms and Dartford. I read all the available literature on Leatherhead. A couple of days before the road opened I called up Tony and told him what I was planning.

'That's a brilliant idea.'

'You think so?'

'Everyone who drives on the M25 will buy a copy.'

'You reckon?'

'Absolutely. I'm coming with you.'

'Why?'

'You're going into uncharted territory. You need a map reader.'

'I don't need a map reader. I'm going round in a circle.'

'I can be Boswell to your Johnson.'

This wasn't a bad idea. It would be good to have someone to talk to, bounce ideas off. Tony could be annoying in an enclosed space, but he was well read, and saw the world from an oblique angle. He also said funny things which I could steal.

He came round the next evening. We watched the news and Thatcher officially opening the motorway. She said, 'Some people are saying that the road is too small, even that it's a disaster. I must say I can't *stand* those who carp and criticise when they ought to be congratulating Britain on a magnificent achievement.'

'It's uncanny, isn't it?' said Tony.

'What is?'

'How she looks just like your mum.'

We left in the rain the following morning, joining the motorway at junction 18 near Watford. Tony Blackburn was on Radio London. At the news bulletin we were told the M25 was now officially open for traffic.

Open wasn't how it felt. My little VW was hemmed in by HGVs on all sides. A truck from the Royston cesspool-emptying service blocked the way forward. A van from Paxo bullied us on one side, a coach towered above us on the other. The spray was exhausting the windscreen wipers. It was as if we were trapped inside a moving car wash.

'So what's the concept behind this book?' said Tony.

'I'm not sure. I thought I'd start with a look at the story of the M25, the history, the difficulties in planning permission et cetera...'

'I'm bored already. You've got a great idea here and you're going to screw it up.'

'How do you see it?'

'I see it like a journey through a wasteland. The M25 is a desert and you're battling through it, facing your demons. A sort of *Fear and Loathing in West Byfleet*. What's your first line?'

'Dunno.'

'I'll think of a first line for you.'

We passed a sign for London Colney. 'That's where Arsenal train,' said Tony. 'Put that in your book.'

He re-tuned to Radio 1. The Simon Bates show started and the traffic slowed to a standstill as if it just couldn't face going on.

'The M25 was a black serpent...' said Tony.

'What?'

'That's your first line. The M25 was a black serpent... that had swallowed its own tail.'

'That's rubbish.'

'It's a lot better than "Work started on the M25 in 1976 and finished in 1986, £10 million over budget." You need action.'

We drove through the rain towards Potters Bar. Tony said, 'What does Potters Bar mean?'

'What do you mean, what does it mean?'

'You should be finding out what place names mean.'

'It's where there was a pottery.'

'And a bar?'

'Yeah.'

We passed a fox lying on the hard shoulder, its intestines popped out of its stomach.

'And you need to write about the local wildlife too,' said Tony. 'Like it was a jungle trip.'

'Roadkill isn't wildlife.'

'It is on the M25. Squashed mammals are indigenous. "He drove on through the windswept desert of the motorway. The viscera of a fox bloodied the hard shoulder. A kestrel hovered above like a ..." Look, a sign for Theydon Bois. I've never been to Theydon Bois.'

'Neither have I.'

'I don't even know how to pronounce Theydon Bois.'

We came off and drove into the village. There was a pleasant green with a lake, and some Tudor-timbered houses. We bought warm cartons of orange juice from a newsagent and sat outside on a bench. 'The trouble is,' I said, 'I don't have a destination. A goal. A travel book needs to be a journey to the lost land of someone or something.'

'You need to meet some locals,' said Tony.

He meant the two young woman coming towards us with a pushchair. Tony said good morning and asked them how to pronounce Theydon Bois. They giggled and spoke to each other in another language. 'The station is there,' said one of them, pointing to an Underground sign.

'They don't even speak English here,' said Tony. 'Make a note.'

Back on the motorway we were surrounded by trucks again, this time from all over Europe. 'At least the M25 has an international, exotic feel,' I said. 'It's a bit like the Road of Silk.'

'I need a pee,' said Tony.

'There are no services on the M25.'

'What?'

'They haven't built any yet.'

'A 120-mile motorway with nowhere to pee?'

The traffic slowed again. For 30 minutes we moved at walking pace. 'This is torture,' said Tony. 'All these truck drivers are bursting.'

Then for no reason we were rolling again. There were no road works, no accident, nothing. It was as if the traffic had decided: 'Right, that's enough of queuing, let's move at a normal speed again.'

We came off at an industrial estate just before the Dartford Tunnel so Tony could use the toilet. 'Time for lunch as well I think,' he said.

'I've got sandwiches.'

'Forget sandwiches. Wilfred Thesinger didn't carry sandwiches. You need to sample the local cuisine.'

We found a café and ordered egg and chips and tea. Tony said, 'In all the travel books I've read the traveller has a fleeting but passionate affair with a local woman. He falls in love, but then has to leave her, to reach his goal.'

'My chances are slim.'

'You clearly haven't seen the woman behind the counter. She looks like Debbie Harry.'

'No she doesn't.'

'Imagine Debbie Harry without the make-up and the blonde hair.'

'And smelling of bacon.'

'This is Essex.'

'You know what, I feel we're just scratching the surface here. I don't feel I'm getting to grips with the essential M25.'

'Maybe what we're looking at is a postmodern travel book. The destination is wherever the reader wants it to be.'

'I need a focus.'

'Oh shut up. We'll find you a focus.'

We pressed on through the Dartford Tunnel. At least we couldn't hear Simon Bates any more. We never saw the Thames, no sign of water anywhere. When we surfaced from the darkness we were in Kent, and the sun was out, making the asphalt steam. Now there were views and hills. We overtook a hay-truck trundling along in the slow lane, leaving a trail of straw and dust. Steve Wright came on the radio and played the Beatles: 'Let's all get up and dance to a song that was a hit before your mother was born.' We sang along like idiots as Orpington appeared on the signs.

'Ah, Orpington,' said Tony. 'It's sort of proof, if proof were needed, that travel broadens the mind.'

Orpington looked like a suburban experiment, as if 1930s town planners had used it as a guinea pig. Standing in the wide high street it was hard to feel anything but disconnected. I said, 'You know what Orpington needs? It needs Christmas lights. All year round.'

'I want a souvenir,' said Tony.

He bought a postcard of the bus station and sent it to his aunt in Cardiff.

We continued through the deep south: Reigate, Redhill, Leatherhead. 'By this stage in the story,' said Tony, 'we should be travel-hardened. We should be used to the water and the strange food, have a good grasp of the language and be striding along, making good progress. But then suddenly...'

'What?'

'Something happens that changes everything.'

'What?'

'Some chance meeting, a wrong turning taken, a breakdown. You rear-end someone and end up having a passionate affair...'

'How about a cream tea at RHS Wisley?'

'That might do it.'

Wisley smelt of compost. Everything had been cut back for the winter. But this didn't matter; Wisley in October was defined by its leaves – reds and golds and oranges – that created a splash of autumn wherever you looked. We were the youngest people there. The rest were coachloads of elderly folk gathered in the café eating scones.

Outside, the coach drivers were sitting on a bench having a smoke. We told one of them we were doing a circumnavigation of the M25, and he nodded as if it was a perfectly normal thing to do. He said, 'My son helped build the M25.'

'What did he do?'

'He worked on the viaduct at Berry Lane. Near Rickmansworth.'

'We'll look out for it.'

'It won an award.'

'For what?'

'It's got slender piers which nicely blend with the surrounding trees. Apparently. It won an award from the Concrete Society.'

When we got back to the car both Tony and I knew it. We had our goal, focus and destination all wrapped into one.

The skies filled with jets as we passed Heathrow and the traffic grew heavy again at the M4 and M40 junctions. We drove in a convoy to junction 18. There we came off again and retraced our way back through countryside to Berry Lane, and stopped right underneath the skirts of the motorway.

The traffic rumbled overhead on the great concrete slabs of the award-winning viaduct. We examined the slender piers supporting it.

'What do you reckon?' said Tony.

'I'm no expert on concrete piers.'

'I think they're good,' said Tony. 'Expressive and yet understated.'

'Yeah, I suppose...'

'There's no plaque or anything, is there?'

'Can't see one.'

'I mean, you'd think if this was like the Sistine Chapel of concrete viaducts, there'd be a plaque.'

A rabbit hurried past and dived into some brambles. Despite the roar of the traffic it felt like a wild place under here, as though we had found somewhere undiscovered. I said: 'You know what the trouble with this book is? We're looking for meaning in the M25. But it's not like that. There is no goal, no destination. It's the motorway to nowhere.'

'What are you saying?' said Tony.

'I'm saying...we need to come back tomorrow and do it all over again. Maybe anti-clockwise this time.'

Chapter 15

Classic Mistake

Suddenly I had a hit. I was in the bestseller lists. Not with the M25 book. No one other than Tony liked that idea. Publishers thought I was mad. Why would anyone buy a book about the M25? The road was synonymous with pain. I was ahead of my time, that's all. Eventually the M25 developed its own sub-culture: Chris Rea wrote a song about it ('The Road to Hell'); you could take a coach trip round it with the Ironic Coach Tour Company; the M25 won the Radio 4 listeners' poll for the Most-hated Place in Britain. It became the playground of rich boys who would race their Lamborghinis round it at night; and, of course, in time a book was written about it: Iain Sinclair did a circumnavigation on foot.

Walking rather than driving is how we like our travel writing. My book was about a long-distance walk. Cars were only mentioned to be blamed for making us lose our sense of distance, which was exactly what walking restored. So really mine was an anti-car book. And what did I do with my first royalty cheque? I bought a car.

And not just a banger. I had a bit of money at last. I could buy the car I wanted, within reason. I recognized this as a milestone in my life. I could join contemporaries who had climbed on the career ladder long before me and were driving Audis and Golfs. A friend lent me her BMW to try. For a fortnight I drove round in sunglasses with the stereo up loud and the sunroof open. I drove it down to Dorset and my father took one look at it and said exactly what I would have expected: 'Nothing says more about a man than his car.'

'It's not my car. I just borrowed it.'

'Good job.'

But I knew what he meant. I didn't feel comfortable with a BMW either. It made me self-conscious; I blushed when someone looked at me behind the wheel. I parked outside a trendy café in Notting Hill Gate once and a woman gave me the eye, but it wasn't a sexy eye, it was an eye that said: 'Have you nicked that?'

So I searched for the car that suited me; a car that would reflect how I felt about life; a car that was a political statement; a car that said I was on the lookout for a girlfriend. I thought I'd found it when I went to the cinema and saw *Back to the Future*. Michael J Fox was the hero of the film, but a car, the DeLorean, had the starring role. Here was a machine with gull-wing doors and a low-slung stainless steel body. It was built by an American maverick who, after convincing the British government to give him a million pounds of Northern Ireland development money, quickly went bankrupt, got busted for drug-trafficking and disappeared with what was left of the cash. But in between he did manage to produce a car that looked as though it had driven straight off the set of *Thunderbirds*. DeLoreans were the kind of cars we drew at school when we were asked to imagine the year 2020, a time when we assumed we would eat nothing but nutrition pills, wear disposable clothing and drive machines with wings. The DeLorean didn't actually fly, but in the movie it travelled back in time, which was actually more impressive.

Unfortunately it came with a futuristic price tag, to which even my substantial royalty cheque couldn't stretch. I wasn't to be outdone. I went back in time anyway. I eschewed the modern motor car and all its false imagery and went retro or, more accurately, classic. I bought a 1964 Triumph Vitesse in British Racing Green. It had six cylinders, overdrive, a convertible top and a walnut dash, and I fell for it the moment I set eyes on it. The vendor didn't have to sell me anything. I gave him the money without a quibble. I pulled away with a roar and a smirk. It broke down on the M3 as I drove it home.

The motoring age was now old enough for people to be nostalgic about the cars they grew up with. Old Ford Pops were collectable. Cars that always looked a bit silly when they were first launched, like the Ford Anglia with the sloping rear window, were now looked upon with affection. Enthusiasts bought them and restored them, and lovingly polished the chrome which had all but disappeared from modern cars. Clubs started up for devotees to get together and show off their vehicles. They had their own magazines, one down from the top shelf, with full frontals of Austin A35s.

'A Vitesse is a tricky car to look after,' said my local mechanic, 'one for the enthusiast.' He had a garage at the end of my road, and had been recommended by the two women who lived next door to me. Only later did I discover this was because they thought he looked like the singer from Duran Duran.

'You've got to have patience with a Vitesse,' he said. 'You need to develop a relationship with it.' He closed the bonnet. 'You need to spend a lot of money on it.'

He was trying to tell me I'd been sold a load of trouble. He got it going again, but as he wrote out my considerable bill his face screwed up with a 'This car is more trouble than it's worth; don't bring it here again' look.

Fine. I could become an enthusiast. I could learn about engines. How difficult could it be? They always said the great thing about cars from the sixties was they were easy to fix. I bought a Haynes manual and stayed up late looking at all the pretty line drawings and learning about my emission control system. Each Saturday I would walk round the car with a notepad making a list of all the things that needed doing, and then spend the rest of the weekend not doing them.

It kept losing power. The brakes pulled it into the kerb. It vibrated like a washing machine if I drove over 50. My determination quickly turned to frustration. I started to resent the car. Then I started to hate the car. Then I started to hate myself for not being able to fix it. One afternoon I was driving up the A1 when all power went. The thing just stopped. I pulled over and opened the bonnet, knowing that no matter which angle I looked at the engine from, I wouldn't be able to fix it.

I was torn between two options: 1) walk to a phone box and call a breakdown truck; 2) set fire to it and try and claim insurance. The latter option was seeming more attractive when a car pulled up and out jumped two young men.

'Nice,' said one.

'Very nice,' said the other.

'1600?'

'Yes,' I said. 'Want to buy it?'

They laughed, thinking I was joking. 'I had one of these once,' said the first lad. 'Went like shit off a shovel.'

Within minutes they had identified the problem. I didn't understand it then and don't now, but the upshot was I needed a new battery. They towed me to the nearest garage and we slipped the new battery in and everything was fine again. 'You should come to the club,' said one of them.

'What club?'

'The Triumph Owners Club. We meet once a month.'

'And we have a barbecue.'

At last I had found the Samaritans for people who are no good at fixing their cars.

The Triumph Club met in a pub in Enfield. The lads who had come to my rescue introduced me to Neville, who was club chairman and in charge of the burgers that day. I told him about my various mechanical problems and he spoke to me like a doctor.

'And how long have you been having these vibrations?'

'Ever since I bought it.'

'I see, and have you looked at the universal joint?'

'Er... no.'

'I see. Well I think we can help you.' He turned the burgers methodically. 'Come and listen to the talk from our carburettor expert.'

The specially invited carburettor expert spoke for an hour on the joys of a Solex. Some people took notes;

others looked up at him as if he were a guru. Despite his jacket with leather patches and shirt with a frayed collar, I suspected he could have slept with any woman in the room.

There was something of the self-help group about the Triumph Club – 'my name is Dave and I'd like to marry my Triumph'. It pretended to revolve around engines and lectures on mechanics, but in fact the attraction of meeting with other obsessives for Midsummer Madness Camping Weekends and endless barbecues was much more important. This didn't bother me. I became a member that night and paid my subs in full. The club was full of people who were just dying to help me get my Triumph into tip-top condition.

The Triumph Vitesse was introduced in 1962 as a faster version of the Herald, to take advantage of the new motorways. Or so Ralph told me when he came round to my house with his impressive tool-kit. He was under the Triumph in a flash. He was mildly agoraphobic, he confessed to me later. He felt safer underneath a vehicle.

He was going to replace the universal joint, he said. I tried to help by passing him tools like a nurse would to a surgeon. But I got the impression he liked to work alone. He only called me over to have a look when he'd finished something. 'There. You could eat your lunch off that,' he'd say.

He took a break every hour and a half for a cup of tea, and at one o'clock on the dot he said, 'I'm feeling peckish; how about a barbecue?'

'I don't have a barbecue.'

He was appalled at this news. He looked like he might put his tools back into the box and go home.

'But... next door does.'

I ran to the corner shop bought some burgers and went round to the women next door. They had a barbecue in their back yard. 'A mechanic!' they cooed, imagining all mechanics looked like pop stars.

We cooked the burgers and took them to Ralph, who ate them with engine oil smeared over the bun.

'I've got a Citroën,' said Lucy.

'What model?' said Ralph.

'It's yellow.'

The girls made Ralph uneasy; he became clumsy and started to drop things. 'Better get back to it eh? Universal joints don't replace themselves. Got any dessert?'

I ran out and bought a Bakewell tart. Ralph ate it under the car. He was happiest there.

He replaced the joint and overhauled the propeller shaft. 'There you go,' he said when he was finished. 'You could eat your lunch off that.' He suggested I get Nick to come over and look at the fuel and exhaust system. 'Odd sort of bloke, Nick. Prefers Solex carburettors to Stromberg, but it takes all sorts.'

Nick came round. He was no more odd than Ralph or, I suspect, anyone in the Triumph Club. He overhauled the fuel and emission system. I barbecued him chicken legs with a coleslaw salad and treacle tart for dessert.

Brian and his wife Annette came round the following weekend and had a good look at the gearbox and overdrive. Annette oversaw the barbecue. 'Brian likes his spare ribs a certain way,' she said. She produced a fruit salad for dessert

'Brian's on a diet.' Halfway through the afternoon Neville the club chairman arrived. 'Didn't want to miss out,' he said, and got to work on the brakes.

Within a couple of months my Vitesse had been transformed. The engine purred, the rattles were gone. The brakes were true. I polished the walnut dash and put a tin of barley sugars in the glove compartment.

The girls came with me on an outing to the coast. We cruised along the seafront at Margate and pedestrians stopped and pointed. At some lights a van pulled up alongside and the driver called, 'I used to have one of those.' I felt proud. I felt the Vitesse said something about me. The restoration had taught me a lot; not much about mechanics, but I reckoned I could cook the best barbecue in our street.

The girls went on the beach. I stayed in the car park and answered questions asked by the nerdy men who gathered round the car.

When the girls got back I made them brush every grain of sand from their feet before they got in. 'Prat,' said Paula.

I went away on a travel-writing trip to Turkey. There I met an American family who lived in London and asked me to dinner when we got back. I drove the Vitesse with the top down and parked outside a good address in Holland Park. I thought I'd met the whole family on holiday but there was a daughter, Catherine.

'They never mentioned you,' I said.

'A whole week and they never mentioned me!'

She came outside with me as I left. The Triumph was

waiting there in the glow of the street light. I climbed in and started the engine. A throaty rumble rose into the summer air. I asked for her number.

'What?'

I switched off the engine so she could hear me. She wrote her number on the back of my hand.

Our first date was to be an evening walk and then a drink in a country pub. I parked the Vitesse outside my flat. I cleaned it and polished it. I was careful to put on a shirt that didn't clash with the British Racing Green.

I was standing at the window, waiting for her to arrive, when I saw a beat-up, left-hand-drive Fiat with Greek licence plates pull up and park behind the Vitesse. I felt peeved. A car like that spoiled the view. Then I saw it was her. I looked at the Fiat more closely. It was filthy and dented in many places. A wheel hub was missing and the aerial was a coathanger. All of those things could have been forgiven, but then she did something that made me shudder. She got out and kicked the door shut.

We drove out in the Triumph to Ayot St Lawrence, near to the house where George Bernard Shaw had lived. When we pulled up I jumped out and ran round to open the door for her, then gently closed it, trying to set a good example. 'You English,' she said.

It was a long and warm summer's evening. We walked and talked for two hours, then went to the pub and had sausage and chips. We drove home in the dark, the Vitesse's six cylinders echoing down the high-sided country lanes as I flipped it into overdrive. When we got home I was out in a flash to open the door for her again. 'How come you open the door for me when I get out, but not when I get in?' she said.

I smiled. 'It's been a lovely evening.'

We had lovely evenings through the rest of the summer. Catherine liked the Vitesse well enough, although I didn't think she fully appreciated it, or the work that had gone into it. Cars were just machines to her; a means of transport.

I noticed her kicking the door shut on the Fiat on a number of occasions – in fairness she was usually carrying piles of work papers out of the car and didn't have her hands free. I never mentioned it though. How can you tell a woman that you like everything there is to like about her except the way she kicks her car door shut, and if you ever catch her kicking *your* car door like that, the relationship is over?

Only once did I react to the way she treated her car, the time she was reversing into a parking space at the supermarket and she backed into a barrier. I yelped: 'Oh no!'

'What's the matter?'

'You just crashed.'

She got out and headed off to the store.

'You're not even going to look?'

'At what?'

'The damage!'

'What's a bumper for?'

I took a look. She'd dented the side panel as well as the bumper.

'It's not just the bumper, it's also the wing.'

'What's a wing for?'

I didn't take Catherine to my Triumph Club meetings, but I kept going throughout the summer. I felt I owed it to the other members. They liked to keep an eye on the Vitesse. Ralph would come over and put his ear to the engine. Neville would ask me questions like: 'Have you noticed any unusual discharge?'

They insisted I come to a Triumph rally with them. We met in a Little Chef on the A5 and motored in convoy to a field in Bedfordshire where all manner of Triumphs had gathered with their owners standing proudly by them. You were supposed to lift your bonnet so other enthusiasts could peer in and ask questions about your rebuild. A man said to me, 'Just out of interest, what method did you use to withdraw the vertical link and outer drive shaft on the rear axle?'

'The usual.'

A Dutchman, who said he was from the Eindhoven branch of the Club, asked if I'd start my engine. 'Sure,' I said, and he listened to it for a while and then said, 'Do you mind if I record it?' and he pulled out a little tape recorder.

'Be my guest,' I said, and he put on some headphones and happily recorded the sound of my engine for ten minutes.

'Want to hear it?' he asked me afterwards. I took the headphones, and sat and listened to my own car's engine, and it sounded like poetry.

It was as I drove home that evening that I began to wonder if there was something missing in my life.

I felt so indebted to the club members for all the work they'd done on my Vitesse that I suggested I throw a celebratory barbecue to thank them all. 'That's very kind,' said Neville. 'Let's make it part of our end of summer event: a treasure hunt this year.'

This was arranged for a Sunday in September. I didn't tell Catherine, but she opened my fridge and found it stuffed full of meat. 'Having a party?'

'A little get-together.'

'Great.'

'It's the Triumph Club, nothing interesting.'

'I've never met your friends from the Triumph Club.'

'No.'

I was being evasive which just made her keener. I said, 'You wouldn't like it, it's all about cars and engines, and there's a treasure hunt before the food...'

'I love treasure hunts. I'm coming! I'm a great map reader.'

We all met in the Little Chef on the A5 again. There was a good turnout. The cars looked pristine, many with hoods down, many with bonnets opened as the drivers tinkered. I introduced Catherine, and all the members said hello without establishing eye contact, then offered to show her their engines.

Neville handed out the clues for the treasure hunt. 'What's the prize?' asked Ralph.

'Ten litres of radiator fluid,' said Neville.

The treasure hunt was straightforward. A list of clues led you round the countryside from one landmark to the next, until we got back to Neville's house where his wife was standing by to fire up the barbecue.

We set off at ten-minute intervals. Catherine read the first clue: '"Left at the lights and then a holy lane, I live in the sea, and I'm also vane." Simple. We need a church with a weathervane that's a fish.'

'Very good.'

But we couldn't find a church, with a weathervane or without one. 'You have to turn left,' said Catherine.

'There is no left.'

'There must be a left eventually. You can't have no left.'

We drove for five miles. No left. We stopped and asked a couple walking along the road with their dog if there was a left turn nearby.

'There's a left one back the way you came.'

'That's a right turn.'

'No it's definitely left.'

'Are there any churches nearby', asked Catherine, 'with a weathervane on top that's a fish?'

They thought carefully. 'St James, in Little Netherton.'

'That's a Methodist chapel.'

'No it isn't.'

'Yes it is.'

We drove on to Little Netherton. The chapel had been converted into flats. We drove on to the next village. There was a church but the weathervane was a ship.

'Ships live in the sea,' I said.

'Sunken ones do.'

'Oh come on.'

I was about to drive on when Catherine said, 'Stop; turn it off.'

I turned off the engine. 'Listen,' she said.

I could hear the cylinders hiss then let out a little sigh.

'Can't you hear it?'

There was music, strings, coming from the church.

We went inside the flint building to find a quartet playing. There was an audience small enough for our entry to make everyone turn. Someone handed us a sheet of paper with the programme on. 'Bartók,' said Catherine.

'Great.'

I'd never heard Bartók before. It sounded raw and difficult to listen to, but every now and then there were glimpses beyond the atonal fog into a beautiful and sunlit land. I wanted to leave, but then I had to stay, and before I knew it an hour had gone by.

We came out blinking in the sunlight, but calm now, and suddenly the day was hopeful. Someone from the concert was looking at the Vitesse. He said, 'Is this the model with the single or double valve springs?'

'I haven't got a clue.'

We made it back to Neville's. The others had all returned long before us. 'Where have you been?' they asked. They sounded worried, but this was because I had the food for lunch in the car.

'I'll get the meat,' said Catherine.

Neville said, 'I like her. I think she'll be a valuable member of the club in time.'

I watched Catherine as she opened the car door and took out the cooler. It was a heavy box without a handle.

'Bring her to club night next week,' said Ralph. 'There's a talk on ignition systems.'

Catherine managed to lift the cooler out, but now her hands were full and she had no way of closing the door.

'Leave the door!' I screamed, too late.

In slow motion I saw everyone turn to see Catherine kick the Vitesse door shut.

There was a silence. Ten Triumph Owners Club members stood with their mouths open, aghast. Catherine stood there holding the cooler. 'What?'

Neville looked at her as though she'd just urinated in the fish pond. Then he looked at me as if to say: the only reason I don't throw you out is because we haven't had the barbecue yet.

I knew then that Catherine had to go.

There was an alternative, of course. The car could go. This radical idea came to me later in the week when the idea of going to Club night filled me with anxiety.

Instead, Catherine and I went to hear a concert. She drove in her Fiat. When I got out I kicked the door shut. I felt liberated.

I sold the Triumph a few months later. A young man came round to buy it. I told him, 'This is an enthusiast's car. You need to know what you're doing.'

'I can soon learn,' he said.

I gave him the keys. He gave me an envelope of cash – more than I'd paid for it; the Vitesse had gained in value even in the short time I'd had it. Classic cars were an investment if nothing else.

The lad climbed in and started it up and grinned at the sound of the engine. 'Why do you want this car?' I asked.

'It's... me,' he said.

'You think it's going to get you a girlfriend, don't you?'

'Maybe.'

'Don't worry, you'll be all right.'

Chapter 16

Going Swedish

Catherine's Fiat failed its MOT and she decided to scrap it. She kicked the door shut one last time.

'I'm always the last person to own a car,' she said.

A friend had a second-hand Saab for sale and she agreed to buy it over the phone. I was astonished. I said to her, 'You don't buy a car without looking at it.'

'Do you know about cars?'

'No.'

'Neither do I.'

'I know but...'

'So I just buy a car off someone I trust.'

That made sense. But she was buying a car she might not even like. To begin with, it was an automatic.

'What's wrong with an automatic?' she said.

There was nothing wrong with an automatic, although at the back of my mind I could hear my father saying, 'The day I buy an automatic is the day I stop driving.'

'It's good to shift gears,' I said. 'That's what driving's all about.'

She pulled a face. 'Gears are a man thing.'

I was also suspicious because it sounded too good to be true: a Saab with low mileage, 12 months' MOT, apparently in good condition with a service history, and it was a snip.

'Guess I got lucky,' she said and went off to pick it up.

I was only being difficult because, although it was going

to be her car, I would be driving it too. I'd come to the conclusion I didn't need a vehicle. When I went on my trips I either flew or used the train. My Triumph had been little more than an ornament and rarely used. So we decided we would car-share, which was such a grown-up solution it gave me sleepless nights and commitment issues.

When she came round to my flat later she wasn't so upbeat. 'What's the matter?' I said.

'Nothing.'

'You've been sold a dud?'

'No.'

'It's riddled with rust?'

'No.'

'What is it then?

'It's just that it's... well...'

She took me outside. There it was, a solid-looking, rust-free, well-maintained Saab, as described. What hadn't been described was the colour.

I squinted at it. 'What colour is that?'

'Lime green.'

'That's not lime green.'

'It's not, is it?'

'It's sort of...'

'Vomit colour?'

'I was going to say bile.'

The Saab turned out to be an excellent vehicle. It was sturdy, reliable and comfortable with the kind of features I'd never had in a car before: electric windows, sun roof, rear seat belts. And yet the only comment anyone ever made about it was: 'Yuck.'

It looked like a stagnant pond parked outside the house. People turned round as you drove past and cringed. Pedestrians on zebra crossings would stop and peer in, wondering who was driving such a sickly car.

Catherine did her best to disguise it. She quickly managed to make it her own by reversing it into a few lampposts, scratching it on fences, never washing it. But she could never manage to camouflage the intensity of the swampish green that in the right light was a danger to approaching traffic.

Friends reluctantly accepted lifts; no one parked near it in the street. Once I was sent to Devon to do a travel piece for *The Sunday Times*. I remember driving down the motorway in the fast lane, radio on, eating up the miles effortlessly, thinking: this is the best car I've ever had. But when I got to the hotel the manager came running out: 'You can't park that thing there.'

'Why not?'

'There's a man from *The Sunday Times* coming.'

The only person who didn't react strongly to the colour was my father. 'Good car you've got there,' he said, opening the bonnet and checking the levels. 'Foreign, but good foreign.' Scandinavian was the acceptable face of car imports.

'What about the colour?'

'Lime green, isn't it? Very nice. I had a cardigan this colour once.'

'It's automatic,' I said.

He sighed. 'You'll learn that life is about compromise.'

Just as my mother was relieved to see me in a good,

stable relationship, so my father was relieved to see me in a good, stable car. And that was the Saab all over: stable, sensible. We drove round Scotland in it and it was the perfect touring car. I bought a house and used it to move all my stuff in. I bought a bunch of wood from the DIY shop and strapped it all to the roof rack. Everything about it was practical and dependable, and slowly we even got used to the colour.

'It's good to be the owners of a car this colour,' said Catherine.

'How do you work that out?'

'Because we get to sit inside and so we don't have to look at it.'

That sounded like a positive, grown-up outlook, and the Saab was a grown-up car. I thought it would go on forever. I wasn't prepared for what happened.

I'd never worried about car accidents before. I never imagined that when I went out for a drive I was going to have a smash, end up in hospital or worse.

We'd dealt with all that road safety business. Back in 1966 eight thousand people were killed on British roads, but with high-profile safety campaigns like 'Clunk click, every trip', and drink-driving adverts so graphic some had to be withdrawn, the annual fatality rate had dropped to five thousand by the mid-eighties. Driving was still the most dangerous way to get anywhere, but car accidents happened to other people.

I'd been out with some friends in a pub in Finsbury Park. Catherine was working late and said she'd join us on her way home. It got to ten o'clock. 'She's always late,' I said.

We had another drink. It was getting late even for her. It got to closing time and my friends had to go. 'Hope she's all right,' they said.

'She must have been held up, that's all.'

I waited a little longer. I had no way of reaching her, so I set off to walk over Crouch Hill to her flat. For the first time I wondered if something might be wrong.

There were no lights in her windows and no answer. I sat on the doorstep and breathed a cloud in the chilly night. In the past whenever anyone was late I just assumed that they'd gone off to do something else, or simply forgotten. But now, for the first time in my life, I had someone to worry about. I quickly discovered that if someone you love is an hour late and there's a car in the equation then it's not hard to conjure up images of tragedy. The idea that car accidents happen to other people becomes facetious. Suddenly they are a very real part of our lives. We read about them constantly: motorway madness, multi-car pile-ups. We all know someone who has been injured in a car crash.

I went for a walk round Crouch End, along the route she would have taken home, heading up to the Archway Road, looking out for a shock of lime green to come into view.

A police car tore past, lights flashing, siren screaming, heading off towards the motorway. I decided to let myself be convinced she'd had an accident, on the grounds that the more you catastrophized an event the less likely it was to happen. I imagined a car colliding with her at a roundabout; I saw an ambulance and police, maybe a fire engine with floodlights and cutting equipment.

This wasn't doing me any good. I walked on. It started to rain and I sheltered under the awnings of an all-night garage. I'd had nothing to eat, but the attendant was locked up inside his booth for the night. He shook his head at me. The garage forecourt had 24 pumps but was empty and looked desolate. l longed for the comfort of Mr Goodall and the Green Shield Stamps of my childhood. This was an adult garage, and London was suddenly a very adult place, a world of worry I had gone and got myself wrapped up in.

I walked a loop, but when I got back to her flat there was still no sign. It was now past one o'clock. I hunched up in the doorway, the rain falling hard on the pavement. I tried to fall asleep and that was when I heard the rattle of a taxi pulling up.

I didn't dare open my eyes in case it wasn't her, but then there she was walking up the path. She looked pale and exhausted. I said: 'Where's the car?'

She'd had a proper accident. Another car had run through a red light on the Seven Sisters Road and hit her hard on the driver's side. No one was injured, but the police were called and she'd spent the evening filling in forms. I couldn't understand how she wasn't hurt, but, whereas the other car was a concertinaed wreck, the Saab had protected her.

We went to see it the next morning on the street where she'd left it. The wing and bonnet were buckled, oil had pooled under the engine; the chassis had taken a hammering, but had stood firm. It looked bad, but I felt proud of it. This ugly duckling of a car had saved her life. I felt like patting it and saying, 'Well done, boy.'

We got an estimate for the repairs. 'Is it really worth it?' said Catherine.

'It's a good car,' I argued.

It was a month in the garage. When it finally came home it still looked bruised, its greenness perhaps a little more pale, but still dominating the street.

I tried to look after it. I checked its fluids. I bought new hubcaps as a coming-home present. I watched Catherine head off to work knowing she was in safe hands.

But the car wasn't the same. The engine began to grunt; the boot wouldn't close properly; the sun roof started to leak and the electric windows jammed. It was in and out of the garage and each time the mechanic would shake his head a little more sadly. Then oil started to pool again. He put on a sincere voice and said, 'I think you'd better come into the office.'

He sat me down. 'It's a blown head gasket, I'm afraid.'

I nodded.

'We can fix it but... maybe it's kinder to...'

'I understand.'

I parked it outside her flat. 'I told you all my cars end as scrap,' she said.

'Isn't there a sanctuary that looks after much-loved cars, like they have for donkeys?'

It was November and leaves gathered around the wheels. A different coloured car would have been less conspicuous, but before long her neighbours were asking when it was going to be moved.

A man from a breaker's yard came and had a look. 'Twenty-five quid,' he said.

'We were hoping for 50.'

He laughed. 'Car this colour, you should be paying me.' I almost slugged him.

We took the £25. The Saab's nose was hoisted in the air and it was towed away.

We hugged. I said, 'I've never felt like this way about a car before.'

'There'll be plenty more cars,' she said.

Chapter 17

Booze Cruise

There were three of us. Me, Duncan and Uncle Ken, who lived in Eastbourne.

Uncle Ken was Duncan's relative, not mine. 'He's all right is Uncle Ken,' said Duncan. 'He knows his way round the superstores. Speaks French too.'

The plan was to drive Duncan's van down to pick up Uncle Ken and catch the 9am ferry.

'Be in Calais by ten,' said Duncan. 'Gives us eight hours. Plenty of time.'

Duncan and I knew each other from our local pub. We were very different, but we had one thing in common: we were both getting married the following weekend and we both needed a good supply of alcohol for the reception. A booze cruise was the obvious answer.

'The thing about Uncle Ken,' said Duncan, as we drove down the A23, 'is he's got a very attractive wife.'

'Aunt Ken?'

'Aunt Kate. I've always really fancied her.'

I didn't know Duncan that well. We played darts together, that was all. On a long car journey I expected to get to know him better, but this was a surprise.

'She's late forties, but she's really kept her figure. And she's sort of vivacious and wears these nice dresses that sort of... you know. If she wasn't my aunt, well...'

There were two things about this that made me feel

uneasy: 1) that Duncan should fancy his aunt at all, and 2) that he should be telling me the week before he got married.

He wouldn't let go of it. 'You wait 'til you meet her. She must be the best-looking woman in Eastbourne.'

There's no way Aunt Kate can live up to such a billing, I thought. But then she did just that. She was very attractive indeed. She wore a pretty dress just as Duncan had said she would, and she had a charm that automatically made you feel better about yourself. 'I'm Ken,' said the insignificant person standing next to her whom I hadn't even noticed.

Uncle Ken was a slim, neat man, who had to live with the fact that he would always be known as that bloke with the really attractive wife.

'No getting up to mischief, you boys,' said Aunt Kate, and she kissed her husband goodbye, then she kissed her nephew and, not wanting me to feel left out, she kissed me too. I couldn't explain how suddenly the day looked brighter.

Crossing the Channel had become big business, a much more commercial and efficient process than the primitive setup of 25 years previously when my parents took us all on our Spanish road trip. Now in 1989, during the high season, more than a hundred ferries a day slipped in and out of Dover, Portsmouth, Poole and other smaller ports down the coast, while beneath our feet all manner of machinery was busy boring the Channel Tunnel.

Holidaymakers who slapped a GB sticker on their car and set off across the continent still made up a substantial part of the business, but it was the day-trip shopping spree that had really boomed. From Dover, day returns to Calais and Boulogne were cheap and easy, and the duty free laws had relaxed so that if you lived on the south coast it could be cheaper to take the car to Calais to do the weekly shop, particularly if you were after alcohol. It was a perfect arrangement for a wedding party, and the trolley dash round French supermarkets had become as much a part of the plans as the stag night.

Soon we were on a boat, watching the white cliffs diminish and the clock tower of Calais come into view. Uncle Ken had a road map that covered the whole of Europe, one page of which was relevant to us. He said, 'I think we should hit the supermarkets in Calais first and then, if there's time, head out of town to one or two little wineries I know.'

Duncan was right, it was good to have Uncle Ken along, and he was enjoying his avuncular role. He sat between us, slipping nuggets of marital advice into the conversation, little tips from a seasoned husband to two greenhorns. 'Have you seen the film *Shenandoah*?' he said.

'No.'

'I've always thought James Stewart got it right when he said to love your wife isn't enough, you have to like her too.'

'That's good,' said Duncan. 'I like that.'

'Very wise,' I said.

When I'd told my father I was getting married his guidance had all been financial: 'You'd be surprised the tax relief you get as a married man.' But Uncle Ken's advice was much more emotional. 'The important thing about a marriage,' he said, 'is it's a complete partnership. As Paul

McCartney said, "And in the end, the love you take is equal to the love you make."'

'That's very good,' said Duncan. 'Can you write that down?'

We got to Calais and began the trawl round the supermarkets and wine warehouses. The car parks were full of GBs, and inside the stores was a wedding planner's ruck. In-laws were already battling it out. There were couples who didn't look like they'd make it past the first anniversary. 'I'm not buying Sancerre.' 'Are you saying my family aren't good enough for Sancerre?' 'No, I'm saying they'd prefer Muscadet.'

Duncan said to me, 'Are you buying Champagne or sparkling wine?'

Uncle Ken stepped in. 'May I suggest Champagne? You only get married once – hopefully – and marriage is about making the effort.'

The van quickly filled up. I bought some cheese and sausage as well. By the time we'd finished it was only four o'clock so we headed out of town to one of Ken's wineries.

We drove south under a clear blue sky over the endless fields of northern France. Uncle Ken said, 'We came on our honeymoon to France,' and I knew Duncan was thinking just what I was thinking: a newly wed and beautiful Aunt Kate in one of her summer frocks being ogled by all the French men.

The winery was further than he thought and by the time we got there it was shut. There were no cars in the car park and a *Fermé* sign in the window.

'*C'est la vie*, I suppose,' said Uncle Ken. We decided to get back for the eight o'clock boat. 'I'll drive if you want,' I said to Duncan, and he was happy to hand over the keys.

We piled back in the van, Uncle Ken in the middle as usual. 'We spent the first night in a little hotel near Rouen.'

I wished he'd stop talking about his honeymoon. It was distracting. I was thinking about Aunt Kate in the silk outfit she'd bought specially for her wedding night as I turned the key in the ignition.

It snapped in my hand.

I held up the broken head, examining it, not quite sure what had happened. The others looked on. You could see cogs turning.

'That's a bugger,' said Uncle Ken.

'Have you got a spare?' I said to Duncan.

'I used to,' he said, which meant he didn't. 'Where's the other end?'

It was lodged in the ignition. 'Got any tools?' I asked Duncan.

'I used to...'

'I've got a screwdriver on my Swiss Army Knife,' said Uncle Ken.

We tried to prise out the broken end, but could get no purchase. And even if we had removed it we would have been left with two bits of useless key.

'I feel responsible,' I said. 'I must have turned it wrong.'

Duncan didn't say anything, implying that was exactly what had happened.

'We need help,' said Uncle Ken. 'The nearest town's a mile down the road. I'll go and phone someone.'

I told Duncan to go with him and I would look after the van. I watched them head off down the long, empty road. It was suddenly quiet. Very quiet. Just me and 250 bottles of wine.

I sang to myself. I put my lips over the broken ignition key and tried to suck it out. I wished I'd learnt French. I sang to myself some more.

They returned an hour later in good spirits. They'd called a breakdown garage. The mechanic's wife had said he was out on a call, but she'd tell him to come as soon as he returned. Ken had also called Aunt Kate, who would pass on messages.

The light faded. The mechanic didn't show. We missed our boat. We missed another boat. We missed the last boat.

'We'll have to sleep in the back,' said Duncan.

'I've got some cheese and sausage,' I said.

'If we're going to eat,' said Uncle Ken, 'I think we should have an aperitif, don't you?'

That sounded like an excellent idea.

'I suggest since the white wine isn't chilled we start with a nice Shiraz,' said Uncle Ken.

He had a corkscrew on his Swiss Army Knife. We washed out some plastic coffee cups, and sat in the back of the van on the wine boxes. 'Here's to happy marriages,' I said, and our plastic cups crinkled in a toast.

'I can think of worse places to break down,' said Uncle Ken, slicing some sausage.

With a couple of glasses of wine inside us things didn't seem so bad. Night fell and there was still no sign of the mechanic, but we didn't care any more. We finished the Shiraz and opened a nice Merlot. 'Goes well with the *chèvre*, don't you think?' said Uncle Ken.

'Personally I think the Shiraz has the edge,' said Duncan.

'A nice blackberry flavour,' I said.

'Tell you what,' said Uncle Ken. 'If that mechanic doesn't show up by 10.30 I'm opening a bottle of bubbly.'

We laughed, but Uncle Ken was serious. At 10.30 on the dot he clumsily opened the Champagne and stumbled as he got up and poured us each a cup. 'To our dear wives,' he said.

'To our dear wives.' Duncan and I crashed our cups this time and Champagne sloshed over the sides.

Uncle Ken downed his in one. 'This is great. I'm glad we broke down. Really. I haven't had this much fun for...' He looked at us. 'Marriage isn't everything it's cracked up to be you know.'

'What do you mean Uncle Ken?' said Duncan.

'Well, you know...'

'What?' I said.

'You have to keep trying to work on the relationship and everything. Sort of run out of things to talk about after a while. So she gives me jobs to do round the house. My weekends aren't my own any more. Marriage isn't much fun,' and he belched. 'Excuse me.'

We were drunk, but stunned into silence. Both Duncan and I were thinking of all sorts of fun you could have with Aunt Kate.

'I mean, that honeymoon, that trip down through France was all right, but she doesn't like foreign travel any more. She insists we go to cathedral cities for our holidays, but I get a bit bored with cathedrals.'

'Are you telling me Aunt Kate hen-pecks you?' said Duncan.

'Yes,' said Uncle Ken.

'You need to be firm, Uncle Ken,' said Duncan.

'I *am* firm,' said Uncle Ken.

'You need to be firmer, Uncle Ken,' said Duncan.

I said, 'Why can't you go on your trips to France and Aunt Kate go on her trips to cathedrals?'

'What, separate holidays?' Uncle Ken had the hiccups now. He spilt some Champagne down his front and poured some more.

'You'd have more to talk about then,' I said.

'She wouldn't let me do that.'

'Are you a man or a mouse, Uncle Ken?' said Duncan.

'I'm a mouse,' said Uncle Ken.

'No you're not,' I said.

'Yes, I am.'

'Bollocks,' said Duncan. 'We're going to take you on a drive through France.'

'When?'

'Now. Soon as we get the key fixed.'

I laughed. 'We've got a van and 250 bottles of wine. Think what a time we'll have.'

'See, we're all up for it.'

It dawned on me Duncan might be serious. 'Are you serious?' I said.

'Deadly serious. Can I be honest here?'

'Of course,' said Uncle Ken.

'My weekends aren't mine any more either, and I'm not even married yet.'

They looked at me, wanting to know what my weekends were like. I couldn't think. Were they still mine? I hadn't got a clue. I couldn't think what days of the week were the weekend.

'Same here,' I said, not wanting to spoil the party.

'We're not standing for it,' said Duncan. 'We're going to hit the road. Tomorrow, first thing.'

'I'm up for it,' said Uncle Ken.

'Well of course you're up for it,' said Duncan. 'You're why we're doing it.'

'Where are we going?' I said.

'France,' said Duncan.

'We're in bloody France,' said Uncle Ken. He was thumbing through his road map of Europe. 'Budapest is a good destination.'

'We're just going to keep driving,' said Duncan. 'Just hit the road and keep driving.'

'Or the other way, St Petersburg.'

'I've always wanted to drive to the end of the road,' I said.

'That's what we're going to do.'

'I mean right to the end. See what's there.'

'That's what we'll do.'

'To the end of the road where there aren't any other roads,' I said.

'We're going to go to the end of the end of the road,' said Duncan.

'I'm definitely up for that,' I said. 'Definitely. The end of the road. I've always...'

'Yeah, all right.'

'What are we going to tell the wives and fiancées?' said Uncle Ken.

'We'll tell them we've gone on a road trip. What's it got to do with them anyway?'

'What about our weddings?' I said.

Duncan looked annoyed. 'You're complicating things. That's what Sophie does.'

'Sorry.'

'She complicates things.'

'Sorry. Pass me the bottle.'

'We leave tomorrow at the crack of dawn. The road trip we always wanted to do. No cathedrals. Just freedom, and lots of wineries.'

'Where are we going again?' said Uncle Ken.

'The end of the road,' I said.

Duncan filled the cups. 'To the end of the road.'

'To the end of the road.'

'Athens.'

'Bless you.'

There was a knock at seven o'clock the next morning. We were all sprawled over the boxes. The van was littered with empty bottles. I opened the door and there was a man in blue overalls.

'*Bonjour.*'

'*Bonjour.*'

'*Je suis le mécanicien.*'

'*Bonjour.*'

Uncle Ken got up and went for a pee in the picnic area. Duncan didn't budge.

I showed the mechanic the broken key and he quickly got it out. Then he gave me and Uncle Ken a lift to the locksmith in town where we got another cut. Duncan slid it into the ignition. It resisted to begin with, but then turned and the van started as if this had all been a waste of time.

Duncan looked at me. I looked at Uncle Ken. Uncle Ken looked at Duncan.

'I need a cup of tea,' said Uncle Ken.

We went back to Calais and caught the 11 o'clock boat.

We drove in silence. No one mentioned our trip to the end of the road. I think we all hoped the others had forgotten.

'We drank a bit last night, eh?' said Duncan.

'Telling me,' said Uncle Ken.

We drove back to Eastbourne and Aunt Kate was there to meet us with a kiss and a hug. 'What an adventure you've had,' she said. 'I hope you two looked after him.'

'Don't worry, Aunt Kate,' said Duncan.

Duncan and I watched as she took Uncle Ken by the arm and led him inside. 'I want you to come in and tell me all about it,' she said, and patted him sharply on the bottom.

'That doesn't look like hen-pecked to me,' said Duncan.

'It doesn't, does it?'

PART 3

HOME
AGAIN

Chapter 18

Baby on Board

When I told my father that Catherine was pregnant, he said, 'Don't you think it's time you joined the AA?'

'Why?'

'Family man now. You need to be well insured. Breakdown, home starts. It's time to get responsible.'

As some people took up hobbies like rambling or gardening in their retirement, my father indulged his obsession with insurance. Everything he owned was insured, from the car to the cat. His house was insured against flood and subsidence and plagues of locusts. The food in the freezer was insured. 'There's a year's supply of bolognese sauce in there,' he said when I mocked him. 'You can't take risks with things like that.'

One holiday to France when he hired a car he actually insured his insurance. If he had a bump and the car hire insurance didn't pay up he was insured back in England.

'You can't trust the continentals with insurance.'

Insurance made him a happy man. He found the very word reassuring. It was a trait I hadn't inherited. Insurance to me meant third party fire and theft and I'd rather push the car home than join a motoring organization.

This didn't go down well at the ante-natal class Catherine and I attended. The instructor split us into gender groups. The women were asked to discuss how they might recognize the onset of labour, while the men were encouraged to consider the similarities between looking after a baby and looking after a car.

We sat in a circle and looked at each other blankly. Then Jeff, a carpet shop manager, said, 'You need to make sure you keep fuel in the tank.'

'Nice one Jeff,' said Mike, a tree surgeon.

'You need to keep it clean and well serviced,' said Dave, who worked for British Gas.

Mike added, 'Looking after a baby is like looking after a car because they both need a good breakdown service.'

We all looked at him. He looked deflated. 'You know... if things go wrong. A doctor for the baby. A motoring organization for the car.'

The others nodded. I said, 'Actually I'm not a member of a motoring organization.'

'What, you don't have any breakdown insurance?' said Jeff.

'No.'

They looked as if they wanted to report me to social services.

On the other side of the room Catherine was getting the same treatment when she said she wanted her baby born in a bath.

The car references didn't stop there. The instructor carefully explained to the men what our role would be in the miracle of birth. While our partners would take care of the cramps, the indigestion, the heartburn, the fluid retention, the high blood pressure and the climactic excruciating pain, our job was to make sure that the car was parked as near to the house as possible, topped up with fuel and ready for the journey to the maternity ward.

This felt condescending at first, but as we got further into the pregnancy I realized what a responsibility it was.

'It's no use,' I said. 'We need a new car.'

'What's wrong with the car we've got?'

'It's not suitable for a birth.'

'I'm not having my baby in the car.'

'How do you know? You could have a quick labour. We could be halfway to the hospital. You want to give birth on the back seat of a Vauxhall Cavalier? I think not.'

'What are you saying?'

'I'm saying it's time we bought an estate.'

I knew that having a baby would have a huge impact on our lives, but it wasn't the emotional or even the financial aspect that worried me so much as the amount of luggage we were going to have to carry around with us wherever we went.

Buggy, cot, bedding, changing mat, nappies and accessories, food, activity centre. A trip to the grandparents would involve the same amount of equipment that adventurers bound for the North Pole roped to their sledge. An estate car was the only option.

The car salesman had probably been watching me a while as I peered inside all the estates on the forecourt. I didn't really mind what make we bought; I was interested in cubic volume. Eventually the salesman made his move.

'Looking for an estate?'

'Correct.'

'Growing family eh?'

'Just starting actually.'

He nodded and smiled and knew he had me. 'I've got a little boy; six months,' and he pulled out his wallet and showed me a picture. An irresistible baby with blond curly hair and chubby arms. 'Just got his first tooth,' he said.

'What car have you got?'

'Oh, we've got an estate, a Peugeot 409, it's perfect: roomy, safe. There's one just over here.'

It was probably the easiest sale he had all year. I drove it home, stopping just once to buy a *Baby on Board* sticker, which I didn't dare put in the back window just yet. I slipped it in the glove compartment ready for the big day.

I was sitting in a queue on the ring road, remembering a science-fiction short story, *The Great Moveway Jam* by John Keefeauver, in which a traffic jam becomes so long and gridlocked that there appears to be no way of ever unravelling it. A wall is built around the jam to stop people abandoning vehicles. Government helicopters air-drop supplies; communities spring up among the stranded vehicles; children go to makeshift schools on the roadside. A year passes. Then one day the helicopters come as usual, only this time it's not food they're carrying, but concrete. The traffic jam is paved over and becomes a road once more.

Britain hadn't quite got to that stage – the government had finally produced a plan for tackling congestion, the 1989 *Roads for Prosperity* White Paper, which announced 'the biggest programme of road-building since the Romans' – but this was little comfort if you were sitting in a jam in the same place every day.

The traffic system where I lived on the edge of London was deranged. We had a ring road, but the narrow streets of the town centre were often so blocked no one could get out to it. Rush hour was a free-for-all. Our street was a rat run and vehicles would tear down it at ridiculous speeds, trying to navigate a way around the chaos.

One day Sid, my neighbour, knocked on the door. He flashed ID and said, 'I'm Sid Collins your neighbour.'

'Yes, I know. You live next door.'

'I'm collecting signatures for humps.'

'Humps?'

'Great lumps of tarmac across the road that slow the traffic down.'

'Okay. I'm up for that.'

Everyone in the street signed the petition, and we couldn't quite believe it when signs went up announcing that speed humps were actually going to be introduced. It was all part of the council's traffic calming master plan that had already seen the pedestrianization of the town centre, complete with ornamental flower tubs and antique lampposts, and the exodus of businesses to the ring road where a community of garden centres, DIY stores and pubs with vast car parks had sprung up. Now it was investing heavily in speed humps. There was even a Humps Hotline you could ring.

One morning a team of road workers arrived with an impressive amount of machinery and by the end of the day neatly contoured hillocks of tarmac had been piled at intervals across the road. The street rejoiced. We had a grand opening with an 11-year-old declaring the humps officially open. Early the following morning we were woken by the sound of crashing milk bottles as the milk float bounced down the street. Then came the screeching of tyres and the thump of expensive suspension as the daily fleet of BMWs came charging through at the usual speed, only now they slammed on the brakes and went up and over the speed humps like a Saracen personnel carrier.

Basically, the humps didn't stop the rat run, they just made it noisier. In time we grew to regret them, then to hate them. One day there was another knock on the door and there stood Sid flashing his ID again.

'Hello, I'm Sid Collins, your...'

'Yes, yes, hello Sid.'

'I'm collecting signatures to have the humps removed.'

It was clear that a complete rethink was needed if the town was going to tackle its traffic hell effectively. Salvation finally came when the council announced it was going to commission a revolutionary one-way system, a design already being used to great acclaim in Gothenburg.

The local newspaper published the plans. Once again Sid was on the doorstep. 'I'm collecting signatures for a campaign against the new one-way system.'

'What's wrong with the new one-way system?'

'It's outdated.'

'It's not been built yet.'

'It's common knowledge that one-way systems actually increase the amount of traffic rather than decrease it.'

Sid planted himself behind a trestle table in the pedestrianized area in town with a sign that read: *One Way: No Sense*. The next week he was back with a sign that read: *One Way: Unfair*. The following week he had a sign that read: *One Way: No Way*. This was his breakthrough sign. His campaign took off and he got his picture in the paper every week. He became a local celebrity and the council asked him to be Father Christmas in Santa's Grotto that year.

I was generally happy with the plans for the new one-way system, until they announced when it was to open. It was the same day as Catherine's due date.

The potential for disaster here was alarming. I had planned my route to the hospital down to the smallest detail, monitoring traffic flow through town at different times of the day. If Catherine went into labour before 7.30am we would turn left at the bottom of our road; after 7.30, we would turn right. If she started in the middle of the night we would go through town. If her waters broke any time between 2pm and 5pm we would risk heading out to the ring road. But now...

'You seem anxious,' said Catherine as she watched me fret over the old and new town maps.

'You don't understand. If the baby is born a day before your due date we have to turn left up Palmerston Avenue and then first right down Anglesey Road. If you give birth on or after the due date, Palmerston Avenue is one-way and we'll have to take Frobisher Road and then Townsend Drive...'

I didn't need this kind of stress. When the midwife came round to check on Catherine's blood pressure I asked her to take mine as well.

'It is slightly raised,' she said.

'How raised?'

'You have the blood pressure of a 60-year-old man.'

Catherine covered her pregnancy with a jumpsuit. The town council covered its new one-way signs with sacking. Meanwhile, I obsessively checked my oil levels. I topped up with anti-freeze. I filled the windscreen washer. The chances of a dirty windscreen sabotaging our trip to the hospital were remote, but I wasn't taking the risk.

Then I purloined two traffic bollards from a nearby road works and whenever I drove anywhere I put them in front of the house to secure the parking place.

Soon Sid was knocking on my door.

'Hello Sid.'

'I noticed you put bollards on the road when you drove away this afternoon.'

'That's right.'

'You can't put bollards on the road.'

'My wife's having a baby.'

'If we all put bollards on the road there'd not be enough room for us all to park.'

'My wife's having a baby.'

'How do you know my wife's not having a baby?'

''Cause you haven't got a wife.'

'I have a renal condition. Mr Broad from 64 has angina. The Knowles at 75 have a child with nut allergies.'

'Your point being?'

'We all might need to be rushed to hospital at any moment.'

I had no idea we lived in such a sickly street.

A week to go and I said to Catherine, 'Tonight would be a good night to have a premature baby.'

'Why tonight?'

'It's a beautiful starry sky, plus there's little traffic, and the car is parked right outside the house.'

She went to bed. I phoned my father. He said, 'Have you got a spare set of keys in case the original set falls down the drain outside your house?'

'I didn't know there was a drain outside our house.'

'Have you joined the AA?'

'Don't be silly.'

'You always liked sailing close to wind.'

That night Catherine woke me with a prod. 'It's started.'

I didn't panic. I calmly dressed and helped her downstairs. She sat in the living room while I took the already packed bags out to the car. The night was still clear and frosty. I remember thinking: what a beautiful night to be born on.

We drove smoothly through town, turning left down Bank Street. But then there was a diversion for road works. It led us down side streets, through parts I'd never been to before. I became disorientated, and then I noticed steam was coming out of the bonnet. The temperature gauge was off the scale. I heard Catherine moan and say, 'My contractions are 60 seconds apart.'

I lifted the bonnet. Oil was everywhere; something had burst. There was no one around, not a light on in a house. Then out of the darkness I could see headlights. A van, a bright yellow AA van. I frantically waved it down.

'Can I be of assistance, sir?'

'My wife's having a baby! I need to get to hospital.'

He examined the car. Then when he heard Catherine moan he examined her. 'Ten centimetres dilated, sir. No time to get to the hospital. I'll have to deliver the baby right here.'

'But you're an AA man.'

'All part of the training, sir. Maybe you'd like to pass me my socket set. You are a member, of course...?'

I woke up in a sweat from that one.

Delivery day minus 1. A Sunday. 'This would be a really good time to go into labour,' I said to Catherine as I brought her breakfast. 'There's nothing wrong with being early, sets a good example, the child will be punctual for everything in life.'

But nothing happened that day, nor that night. I couldn't sleep. I looked out of the window and saw workmen up ladders removing the sacking from the new one-way signs.

All was quiet until dawn broke. Then traffic started to head into town to be met by a one-way system so complicated that by 7.30 all was gridlock. And it stayed that way all morning. A three-hour window of flowing traffic opened early afternoon, but then closed again by 5pm. The queue at the end of our road was at a standstill. Traffic lights changed and nothing moved. If Catherine had gone into labour I would have had to push her through town in the wheelbarrow.

Having spent the previous week encouraging her to give birth, now I tried to persuade her not to. 'Nothing wrong with a baby being a few days overdue, keep people guessing.'

A few days would give things time to settle, let drivers get to know the new system. Or so I thought. But the next day the queues were just the same. And the next day. And the next. Catherine could wait no longer. Early morning four days past her due date her waters broke. I phoned the hospital and was told to wait until contractions were five minutes apart. That happened at precisely 7.20am. Just as the town was about to settle into another day of impasse.

My first big test as a father and I was going to fail.

Our bag was packed. My mid-labour sandwich was all ready. We got in the car and headed off. The end of the road was completely clear.

It was like a miracle, on a scale with the Red Sea parting. The streets were as empty as Christmas Day, as if England was playing a World Cup Final. We drove easily and quickly through town, navigating the new one-way system with ease. We didn't break down. I didn't need the AA. 'I'm glad you bought an estate,' said Catherine as she knelt on all fours in the back. I felt a wave of triumph as I successfully pulled up outside the maternity ward.

'Well done,' said Catherine as I led her inside. Having carried out my part of the operation, now it was over to her.

The midwife greeted us: 'I'm surprised you got there. I parked out of town and walked in. Everyone did.'

It was hard to believe what had happened. The new one-way system had solved the town's traffic problems by causing so much chaos that everyone had left their cars at home and walked in, or had taken the bus. It was a master plan. Brilliant.

Unfortunately, word quickly got round that the town was empty. As Catherine and I spent the day in the birthing pool the streets filled up again. Our baby son arrived into the world and four hours later he was experiencing his first sheer-volume-of-traffic hold-up on the way home.

The intolerable daily jams returned. Drivers never got used to the new system. Market traders complained business was suffering. Sid knocked on the door again. 'Did you have your baby?'

'Yes thank you.'

'Boy or girl?'

'Boy.'

'Maybe he'd like to sign this petition to get rid of the one-way system.'

Within a month the grand system, such a hit in Gothenburg, had been abandoned. One night men from the council came back with their sacking and re-covered the signs. The old ones were put back up. The town reverted to the way it was.

It was as if the planners had played a multi-million-pound trick on us, subjected us to a month of traffic anarchy just to teach us how lucky we were to have our original arrangement.

I took my father's advice and joined the AA.

'One question?'

'Yes sir.'

'Are your patrolmen trained to deliver a baby?'

'No sir.'

'Didn't think so.'

Chapter 19

Snow Day

'We need a four-wheel drive,' said Catherine.

'Why do we need a four-wheel drive?'

'Everyone here has a four-wheel drive.'

Not everyone, but certainly many of our neighbours did. Some were huge and menacing vehicles you'd feel confident going off to war in; others were small and looked like golf carts. But they all proudly displayed the 4WD sign on the back door, and no matter how meek the driver, as soon as he or she got behind the wheel they became fearless.

'I really don't want a four-wheel drive,' I said.

It was the mid-nineties and we had moved with our two boys out of the South East to a village in Derbyshire. The High Peak loomed over us, all gritstone and peat. Wild weather blew in over the hills from the west. Our house looked frail in the face of the wind and hail. And this was summer. What was going to happen when the nights drew in?

Some friends came to visit: 'You'll be back in six months, betcha,' and they drove off up the hill and out, back to the balmy Home Counties, leaving us to the elements.

The farmers laughed and pointed to the pictures on the pub walls of snow drifts blocking the road into the village.

'They're laughing because they've all got four-wheel drives and we haven't,' said Catherine.

It was true, the farmers did have four-wheel drives. But they needed them. They had to tow trailers full of sheep and when they'd drunk too much they had to drive home from the pub across the fields.

'The next door neighbours have a four-wheel drive,' said Catherine.

They did, one with a soft top that looked a bit like a beach buggy. I said to them, 'So how do you find it?'

'Wouldn't be without it. The snow can get pretty bad in the winter. You need to be ready.'

I was ready. I'd bought a shovel. I wasn't a snowfall denier or anything. I just wasn't convinced by the whole four-wheel drive argument. It felt like a marketing exercise. In the past it was only the military that had them; they were purely functional vehicles. But then Range Rovers appeared and established a niche market among the country set. This stretched to Yuppies who had enough money to buy a weekend cottage and needed a vehicle to match. Four-wheel drives came to represent escape from the rat-race, the ability to venture into the interior. They said: even though I work in an office and wear a suit all week, you should see my wild side emerge at weekends. It didn't take long for every major manufacturer to produce one.

But then these weekend wildmen started cruising around in their Shoguns and Cherokees back home in the city. London became a jam of Chelsea tractors, the occupants riding high above the rest of the traffic, their three tonnes of steel nudging their way down Kensington High Street on the school run. Theories about global warming were beginning to gain credibility, but these drivers weren't bothered about their fuel consumption. The four-wheel drive was a symbol of the nineties, a personal statement, and the statement was 'Bollocks to the rest of you'.

Summer turned to autumn. The heather on the moors turned brown; the rowan trees were weighed down with berries. The clocks went back and we had Guy Fawkes night. The weather grew colder, but there was no sign of snow.

The local paper ran adverts: 'Make sure your car is set for winter,' and there was a picture of a woman standing in the snow by her broken-down car while a man in overalls peered under the bonnet. I wasn't worried. I had anti-freeze. I had my window scraper. I wanted to say to everyone: how did we all cope before the days of four-wheel drives?

Our cat got a weepy eye, and a neighbour told me of a vet everyone used. 'He lives on a farm on the moor.'

It was raining hard. The fields were awash. 'You need a four-wheel drive to get up there in this weather. I'd better take you.'

'It's all right. I'll go later in the week.'

'Your cat is not well.'

'It's just a weepy eye; she's had it weeks.'

'She needs to be seen now.'

He had a Discovery with more electronics in it than a space shuttle. Inside was like sitting in your own ecosystem. As we drove along he proudly demonstrated all the features. 'How's your seat temperature?'

'Pretty good.'

'I can change it if you want.'

'No it's fine.'

We sped along with Mozart playing on the stereo. 'Not too loud for you?'

'No.'

'I can control your speaker.'

'Mine's fine. Maybe the cat would like it a bit louder in the back.'

'Okay.'

He switched up Mozart on the rear speakers for the cat.

We drove over the moor, looking down on all the poor wretches who had to travel without cruise control and a double sunroof. Eventually we turned off onto a rough farm track, although up in the cockpit of the Discovery we felt little discomfort, just a ripple or two. When we got out at the farm, however, my friend was appalled at the muck splashed up the side of the vehicle. 'Damn it,' he said. 'Look at that. He should really do something about that track.'

There was nothing wrong with the cat. The eye would clear up on its own, said the vet. The journey had been wasted. On the way back we stopped at a garage and jet-washed the Discovery. 'I'm not going up there again,' my neighbour said.

My son, Francis, came home from school and said, 'I'm the only boy without a four-wheel drive.'

It was December now. Still no snow. The roads got icy occasionally, but the council gritter came out each time and there was no problem.

'That's not exactly true, is it?' I said. 'What about the Whites, and the Gills, and the Taylors?'

'All right, I'm the only cool boy without a four-wheel drive.'

I remembered what it was like at school when your father drove an embarrassing car. 'I'll tell you what we'll do,' I said.

'Buy a Shogun!'

'No. We'll buy snow chains.'

Snow chains seemed like a much more sensible idea and were of course much cheaper. I saw a set advertised and bought them over the phone. I took Francis with me to pick them up. He'd got the idea that snow chains were like caterpillar tracks; he was going to be the only boy to turn up at school in a tank, which was pretty high on the cool scale. When he saw me hand over good money for a plastic bag full of what looked like railings he was appalled. We took them home and fitted them on the Peugeot.

'There,' I said. 'How cool is that?'

It looked like exactly what it was: a home-made four-wheel drive.

Before we moved out of London friends had said, 'You won't have shops round the corner, you know; you'll be driving everywhere; it'll be a two-hour trip to buy a pot of paint.'

But in most cases we found that things came to us. There was a mobile fish van. There was a vegetable delivery service. There was even a mobile hairdresser.

Her name was Lucy. It was written on the side of her opal-coloured convertible Suzuki Vitara. Hair by Lucy. Door-to-Door Service. Perms and Colours.

She came and did all four of us in our kitchen. I said to her, 'A four-wheel drive eh?'

'The truck? Yeah. You've got to have four-wheel drive round here. I can take that anywhere I want. I took it in a field the other day. Took the dog for a walk. I mean I live in Sheffield, but you have some days when it's really slippery. I could take that across Africa.'

She had two-toned nails and henna highlights and didn't look the sort to drive across Africa, but what did I know?

'Four-wheel drives are a lot safer too. If you hit something you always come off better.'

'What happens if you hit another four-wheel drive?'

'Is that enough off the back?'

We booked her to come again in the new year. After she'd gone the whole family looked at me and I knew what they were thinking: even our hairdresser has a four-wheel drive.

I managed to hold out until Christmas when the old Peugeot started to develop something that sounded bronchial. It wouldn't start, then it would start but stopped five miles down the road, which was worse than not starting in the first place. I took it to the garage. I had another one of those head-shaking discussions with the mechanic, then decided to have it put down.

So a new car was needed, and the pressure to buy a four-wheel drive was really on. Francis put it on his Christmas list just below Power Rangers pyjamas. Two-year-old Daniel handed me his list, which was pretty well-written for a kid who couldn't write. That was because Francis had written it and the first item was a four-wheel drive. On Christmas day my present was a pullover and a card that said: 'Go and buy yourself a four-wheel drive.'

So I did. I quizzed neighbours on what make to go for and one of them recommended Subaru: 'Stylish, nippy, powerful, good handling, all-wheel drive.'

'All-wheel drive? What's "all-wheel drive"?'

'All the wheels are driven.'

'All four of them?'

'All four of them.'

'So it's four-wheel drive?'

'I suppose it is.'

I went to a showroom in Matlock. The salesman had a tie with Christmas puddings on it. He said, 'The snow's coming. A four-wheel drive is a very wise investment.'

It would have to be, looking at the prices on the windscreens. 'Is there such a thing as a three-wheel drive?' I asked.

In the end I took my neighbour's advice and bought a Subaru.

'Very sensible,' said the salesman. 'Rally driver's favourite.' As if I was bothered.

All-wheel drive meant that four-wheel drive was engaged all the time, not just when you switched it on, a fact I only discovered when I had driven the Subaru home.

This was a little disappointing. I imagined switching to four-wheel drive would be like going to light speed in *Star Wars*. But it didn't feel any different.

The family came out to inspect it. 'It's not very... big or anything, is it?' said Catherine.

'It's all right,' said Francis. 'Subarus are cool,' and he went back to Power Rangers.

We sat back and waited for the snow. I kept checking the forecast, looking for something Siberian coming in from the east, but we went into January and there was nothing.

The snowdrops came out. The Subaru sat in the driveway yet to be tested. It looked as though we were going to go the whole winter without a flake. But then one evening in February the TV weatherman had a grim face. All the arrows were coming in from the east. The words 'drifting' and 'hazardous', 'heavy' and 'absolutely necessary' were used.

The news quickly got round. Everyone said, 'It's coming. Are you ready?'

'I'm ready. You ready?'

'I'm ready.'

'Good. We're all ready then.'

Next door was outside putting a piece of cardboard on his windscreen. Such an unscientific device looked out of synch with a vehicle that had four different wiper speeds; it was the kind of thing my father did to his cars. 'I need to be off early,' said my neighbour.

Before I went to bed I went outside and saw a starless sky. I looked over at the Subaru and thought: tomorrow's your big day, chum.

It snowed and it snowed, and it snowed some more. When we pulled back the curtains in the morning the whole valley was pristine white. The hills were coated like a ski resort. There were six inches on the shed roof. And it was still falling.

The school phoned to say it was shut for the day. The children jumped out of bed with the kind of enthusiasm only a snow day can inspire. They had breakfast in hats and gloves and were out in the garden building a snowman by 8.30.

Catherine called work. They told her there was no point in coming in because all her clients had cancelled. I went outside and found my neighbour clearing the snow off his car. He looked unhappy.

'I thought you had an early start?'

'They called to say I could work from home.'

There were no car tracks on the road into the village. The gritter managed to get through and it cleared what it could, but no one was going anywhere. We all had a snow day. We spent the morning on the hillside tobogganing, then went back to a neighbour's house for hot chocolate. This was how I hoped winter in the hills would be: not doing battle with the snow, but having fun with it.

Then later in the afternoon there was a knock on the door and there stood a young woman clutching a beauty case in one hand and a handkerchief in the other. She was in tears. I eventually recognized her as Lucy the hairdresser.

'I made it,' she sobbed and collapsed onto the sofa.

She had come to cut our hair. She had left home at 9am,

and for a good section of the journey had managed to follow a snow plough. Then she turned down the valley road. 'It took me four hours. I didn't see another car. I had to use my low ratio gear set all the way. I went into a snow bank and I thought that was it.' We sat her by the fire, gave her soup, supplied her with tissues. Eventually she recovered. She said, 'So who's first?'

We'd forgotten we had booked haircuts for that day, or maybe we never thought she would get through. But since she'd made the effort we lined up.

'Why didn't you reschedule?' I said.

'I've got a four-wheel drive. That's what it's for. I bet the fishman didn't come, did he?'

'No.'

'He doesn't have a four-wheel drive does he? Milkman?'

'No.

'Newspapers?'

'No.'

'I rest my case.'

The only person who went out driving that day was the neighbour who recommended Subaru to me. He drove off 'to test the traction' on his vehicle, which was fine, but then he put the brakes on and skidded into a wall and smashed up one whole side of the car. It seemed four-wheel drives were good for driving in the snow, but when it came to stopping they were the same as any other vehicle.

Those who went to work walked to the train station. The Hope Valley Line was running a good service and they got into Sheffield or Manchester as normal. That was what Lucy the hairdresser did for her return journey. She couldn't face trying to drive across the moor again.

I helped her with her beauty case to the station. She said, 'Think what it was like in the days before four-wheel drives. You would have had to go without a haircut.'

The snow was quickly gone; the roads clear. My neighbour said, 'See, that's why you need a four-wheel drive.'

'Why?'

'To go driving through the snow, up the hill and all over.'

'You didn't go anywhere.'

'I know... but I could have done.'

And that summed it up really. Four-wheel drives spelt freedom, freedom to motor across deserts, to cruise down beaches, to drive into the Badlands and watch the sun go down, to live the dream.

But no one I knew could be bothered.

Chapter 20

Bypass Surgery

As our children grew up I watched for signs that they might be prodigies. Andre Agassi could swat a tennis ball on a string when he was in the high chair. Picasso was working with charcoals aged five. By the age of four my eldest son, Francis, was showing no signs of any special talent, until one day we were driving through town when he said, 'That car's a Honda Accord.'

'Which car?'

'The yellow one.'

I looked and he was right. He knew because the mother of his friend from nursery school picked them up in one. He quickly extended his range, soon being able to tell the make of any car from a distance, the model and engine size as well. 'That car's a VW Golf Turbo 1600.'

'How do you know that?'

He shrugged. 'I just know.'

It was fantastic. I couldn't work out how he did it. I wasn't able to tell cars apart any more; they were designed to look the same rather than different. I decided his was a rare skill, and tried to think of a way it could be harnessed for profit. Could the military use him in any way?

Tony, who was his godfather and keen to teach him to be environmentally aware, tried to encourage him to use these observational powers to spot birds or trees instead.

This wasn't an easy transfer: 'Is that nuthatch a 1.5 or a 2 litre?' said Francis.

Tony's green influence must have made an impression though. One day Francis came back from school with his first project, the kind of homework a dad is just waiting for his child to bring home.

'I have to write about a hero,' he said.

'What hero?'

'Any hero.'

'Freddie Trueman.'

'Who's he?'

'Only the finest fast bowler this country has ever produced.'

His mother intervened. 'Let him choose,' she said.

'You're right,' I said. 'How about Ernest Shackleton?'

'Who?'

'Polar explorer, sailed an open boat across the Antarctic Ocean to South Georgia in 1915. A true hero.'

He wasn't impressed. He went to watch television.

'Don't hijack his project,' said Catherine.

'He'll choose Robbie Williams or someone.'

Later we sat down for supper. Francis said, 'I've decided on my hero.'

We waited with pasta poised on forks. 'Who?'

'Swampy.'

'Did you put him up to this?' I asked Tony on the phone.

'No.'

'He could have done Chuck Berry.'

'Swampy is a hero of our times. Transport policy is a

critical issue and your son is fortunate enough to have a godfather who's an expert on the subject.'

Tony came up for the weekend. He sat Francis down with a pen and paper. 'Okay, why do you want to do a project about Swampy?'

'Because he lives in a tree house and he lives in a tunnel.'

'I see,' said Tony and stroked his beard. 'I think you'll find it useful to include some background to the anti-road movement as a whole, and how the government pressed on with its road-building programme even after one of its own committees reported that more roads just encouraged more traffic and that the way to ease congestion and pollution was to control car use rather than accommodate more.'

'He's seven years old,' I said.

'It's 1997. You don't patronize children.'

'And his essay is only two pages.'

'In that case he also needs to point out how Swampy and his fellow campaigners have had a direct impact on transport policy, to the extent that the Labour party have acknowledged the debt their roads programme owes them.'

'And I want lots of drawings,' said Francis.

'Illustrations are good,' said Tony, and he opened a bottle of wine. 'Right. Let's start at the beginning. Take notes.' And he began to walk round the room.

'When the *Roads for Prosperity* White Paper was introduced in 1989 the government faced little challenge. The nation's love affair with the motorway may have faded with time into a dull marriage, but people still regarded road building and car manufacturing as a sign of growth and were generally in favour... Have you got that?'

'I'm drawing a tree house,' said Francis.

'Good,' said Tony. 'Where was I?'

'The White Paper,' I said.

'But there was an incipient anti-road movement gathering momentum. In London in the early nineties a group named Alarm was helping people protest against plans to build a web of motorways right into the heart of the city.'

'What's wrong with motorways in the city?' I said. 'I love the motorways in the city.'

'I'm sure you do, but as you're cruising along the Westway into the West End, how much thought do you give for the people who live underneath it or the homes that had to be demolished to make way for it?'

'None.'

'Precisely. Before Alarm, if you wanted to protest against a road you went to a planning committee meeting and voiced your concerns, which were duly noted, and then the road was built. But now local people formed groups and lobbied MPs, and what was interesting was they weren't militants. The anti-road movement was successful because it drew supporters from all walks of life.'

'Here's a drawing of a bulldozer!' said Francis.

'Very good,' said Tony. 'This solidarity between campaigners surfaced again in Winchester in 1993, on Twyford Down, where an extension of the M3 to meet the M27 was to be constructed. Rather than build a tunnel under the hill, the plan was to blast right through it, blowing to smithereens a chalk downland.'

'I'll draw a picture of an explosion,' said Francis.

'As work was about to start a small group of New Age travellers calling themselves Dongas made a camp up on the hillside.'

'I'll draw Dongas too.'

'Yeah, all right… But soon local people, outraged at the imminent devastation of the hill overlooking their ancient city, joined forces. The sight of the respectable citizens of Winchester being forcibly removed by security convinced the press whose side they should be on. The land was being ravaged; England needed to be saved from the uncaring bureaucrats; these people weren't activists, they were heroes.'

'But the road was still built,' I said.

'Well of course it was built. That's not the point.'

'What *is* the point?'

'The point is that Twyford taught the protesters how to organize themselves for future campaigns like the Batheaston bypass and the M11 link road.'

'Those roads were built too.'

'Yes. But that's not the point.'

'What *is* the point?'

'The point is that last year when the government started to build the most controversial road of them the all, the Newbury bypass, demonstrators gathered from all over Britain. They made camp in the middle of a condemned woodland, and built an elaborate network of tree houses.'

'I'm going to draw lots of tree houses,' said Francis.

'And a 5,000-strong protest march descended on Newbury.'

'But they're still building the road.'

'Well of course they're building the road. That's not the point.'

'What *is* the point?'

'The point is, getting rid of the protesters has cost 26 million pounds and the government has had enough.'

Tony poured himself another glass. 'Now, this is where it gets exciting. While Newbury was winding up, another protest camp at Fairmile in Devon, battling against an extension to the A30, was preparing for a showdown. This time not only did they build tree houses, they also dug tunnels. When the bailiffs and the police arrived in January, the protesters went underground.'

Tony stood in front of the fireplace for the climax. 'It was freezing cold; they had little food and the tunnels were in danger of collapse. One by one they emerged to the waiting hands of the police and the TV cameras. After a week only one protester remained underground. Eventually they prised him out. Guess who it was?'

He looked at Francis, but Francis was asleep.

Since emerging from his tunnel Swampy had hardly been off the TV. His real name was Daniel Hooper. He was 23 and lived in Newbury, a polite middle-class boy whose mother, far from reprimanding him, gave her support because she thought he was doing something he believed in. Francis cut out a picture of him from a magazine and stuck it on the fridge door.

It wasn't hard to see why Swampy had become a cult figure. He wasn't some lightweight jumping on a bandwagon. He was proud of his claim to have been arrested more times than any other anti-road protester.

Days after he left Fairmile he was in court being fined for damage to security equipment at Newbury. That was commitment.

He was also good on TV, which made him the acceptable face of the anti-road movement. He was cheeky and hobbit-like. And he did have a job. He was an eco-warrior. How cool was that?

We decided on a field trip. We drove down to Dorset to see the grandparents and passed the sites of the protests. As we approached Newbury on the A34 you could see the hillsides clear-cut of their trees, and the diggers at work creating the vast scar across the landscape. A few New Age travellers were parked up in lay-bys. Graffiti was scribbled on signs. We were able to notice all this because the traffic was at a standstill, as it always was around Newbury. There were no easy answers to traffic congestion, but it was the way the government had gone straight for the easiest one that had made the protesters feel justified.

Further down the A34 at Winchester the result of the earlier battle for Twyford Down was there for all to see: a great trench gouged out of the hillside. It was brilliant white from the chalk, and the traffic streamed through the gap, dwarfed by the cliffs on either side.

When it opened, the motorway had made the former Winchester bypass – another notorious bottleneck – redundant. It was closed now and grown wild, and had become a footpath. So it seemed that some good could come out of the new roads. I suggested this to my father as we sat in the garden, the hum from his bypass in the next field piercing the leylandii. But he could see no benefit. He said to Francis he wished Swampy had been around years ago.

'He could have dug a tunnel in this garden and come out right under the road. I'd have been in there with a shovel myself. Your grandma would have supplied sandwiches. Put that in your essay.'

I reminded him of the four-mile queues of traffic that would form on a Sunday evening as everyone made their way back from the coast. Wasn't it worth it to get rid of those?

'You still get four-mile queues on the bypass,' he said.

Francis wrote his project, with drawings of bulldozers and Dongas and exploding hillsides taking up most of the space. He got a smiley face for his efforts. And that should have been that. But we hadn't heard the last of Swampy. One night we switched on TV to watch *Have I Got News For You*, and there he was, sitting next to Paul Merton. It transpired he also had a column in the *Sunday Mirror*. 'The World According to Swampy'. Then the *Daily Express* thought it would be amusing to ask him to dress him up in an Armani suit. Even more amusing, he agreed to do it and got a two-page splash.

His credibility was briefly restored when he went back to the front line, this time heading north to campaign against the building of a new runway at Manchester Airport. It was no use though. He was a celebrity now and the newspapers followed him everywhere he went. The other protesters distanced themselves. It was said that Swampy's tent was like a press office, complete with a bar.

A descent from grace followed. A magistrate in Reading told him to stop 'living off the back of society'. A teenage magazine called him Alternative Totty. Critics came to regard him as an opportunist with a questionable track record. The roads he protested against were built after all; did he and his kind really make any difference?

Perhaps Conservative MP John Watts gave the best answer to that when he said he'd like to see Swampy 'buried in concrete' because of the damage he was doing to the party's transport policy. He was referring to projects like the A329 Guildford to Woking road scheme, which was scrapped on environmental grounds, and the proposed Salisbury bypass, which was postponed indefinitely. What Swampy and his kind had achieved was to turn support for green issues into a vote winner. An election was coming up, and standing next to Swampy or any eco-warrior for a photo opportunity had become an excellent way for a politician to raise his or her profile.

New Labour came to power and eventually abandoned most of the Roads for Prosperity programme. By that time Swampy's 15 minutes of fame were up. A T-shirt appeared with the slogan 'Sod off, Swampy'. Soon afterwards I noticed his picture was gone from the fridge door.

Chapter 21

Pop Top

'I want a caravan,' said eight-year-old Daniel.

'We're not having a caravan. I hate caravans. Everyone who doesn't have a caravan hates caravans. If you have a caravan you have to spend your holiday cooped up with other people who have caravans and I hate people who have caravans.'

'I want a caravan,' said Daniel.

'We're not having a caravan!'

We were discussing family holidays again. I wanted to take the kids hiking with full kit up a mountain where we would camp out and live off the land for a week, returning home bonded and spiritually refreshed. They wanted a caravan. Each option was pure fantasy.

'How about a camper van?' said Catherine, as ever the go-between.

A camper van. Now that was a different thing altogether. A camper van had echoes of the hippy trail, the Summer of Love, the freedom of the road. A camper van was compact and self-sufficient, and it wasn't a caravan.

We hunted around for a suitable model, and eventually found one down a back street in Manchester where an enterprising company did up old VW delivery vans and converted them into campers with cupboards, curtains and drawers everywhere, and, best of all, a roof that popped up to reveal a sleeping compartment for little people.

The boys were in a frenzy of excitement.

'We'll travel all over Europe in this,' I said 'Spain, Italy, Greece.'

'Africa,' said Francis.

'And Africa. Why not?'

'Australia,' said Daniel.

'Yeah, Australia.'

'You know what I'd like to do,' said Catherine. 'I'd like to go to Cornwall and see the eclipse.'

In the summer of 1999 the nation embraced eclipse-mania. It was as good as a royal wedding for the newspapers and merchandisers. You could buy Total Solar Eclipse mouse mats, fridge magnets, wall clocks. Every garage on the way to the West Country warned that if you didn't buy a pair of their protective sunglasses you would go blind. No question.

'It's a once in a lifetime event,' said Catherine. 'The boys will remember it forever. We must go.'

We decided to make a week of it, tour the West Country, land of mystique and legend. Then climb a lonely cliff top and watch the most unearthly display nature has to offer.

To accustom ourselves to our new van, we had a trial weekend in Anglesey. It began to rain the minute we entered Wales and didn't stop for three days. The boys didn't care. A sleeping compartment to themselves was as much fun as they could handle. For the adults the fun factor was less apparent. We sat in a car park overlooking a beach near Holyhead. Catherine read and I listened to the Lord's Test Match as the rain hit the pop-top roof like gravel, and the wind buffeted the vehicle so forcefully I thought it might take off.

The van was very comfortable if everyone else was outside and you had room to move, but when it rained and we were all inside the simplest task involved a mass rearrangement. Getting a saucepan from a cupboard meant you had to lift the back seat, needing two people to stand up and move to the front and the third to lie down in the back so you could unvelcro the cushions and lift a panel to get access to the cupboard, only to discover that the pan you wanted had been stowed in a different place altogether.

We found a place to camp on a farm. The farmer answered his door in his vest. 'Three nights please,' I said.

He took the money and waved his hand at the field.

'Where do we go?'

'Anywhere you like.'

It was a field with sheep in it and nothing else. We parked up against a hedge for shelter. 'Let's play cricket,' I said. And we all stood in the wet field in our anoraks. The sheep watched as we struggled in the long grass for ten minutes before play was abandoned for the day.

But we were prepared for bad weather. We had packed a cupboard full of games. It was so wet we played them all on the first night. By the Saturday we had switched to poker. Teaching young children to play Texas hold'em may not be as edifying as teaching them to observe butterflies, but when you're the only campers in a Welsh field which is slowly filling with water, and there are 36 hours before you're allowed to go home, the rules of parenting change.

We weren't the only people with the idea of heading down to Cornwall for the eclipse. Special coach trips were advertised. All accommodation was fully booked, including camp sites. The police were warning of long queues on the A303. The whole venture was beginning to look unattractive. But then we thought: Cornwall isn't our only option; the eclipse will also be seen across the Channel in Brittany.

Now the holiday took on greater significance. This would be our first continental road trip, and I was reminded of the jaunts my parents had taken us on. I saw myself drawing mileage grids on pieces of cardboard, and sitting at the wheel smoking a pipe, telling the kids to shut up and play I Spy: 'Only a thousand miles to go.'

We booked a ferry crossing from Poole to Cherbourg, stuck a GB sticker on our rear and headed south. The M6 was stuffed. A line of caravans in the slow lane; a line of trucks in the middle. There were special sign-posts on the M5 for Eclipse Traffic. At one services you could buy an Eclipse Special breakfast – a fried egg on toast with a slice of black pudding covering the yolk.

But at Taunton we left it all behind and headed down to Dorset for the night. My father's insurance anxiety had got worse. 'Are you covered for breakdown, theft and collision damage waiver?'

'Of course.'

'How about personal injury?'

'Yes, yes.'

'How much for an arm?'

'What?'

'How much do you get if you lose an arm? Most policies offer £5,000. I don't think it's enough.'

I gave him a tour of the van. He checked the mileage, wrote it down on a piece of paper and handed it to me. 'Keep that safe,' he said.

I said to him, 'I'm looking forward to this trip. I'll always remember those holidays you took us on when we were kids.'

'You enjoyed them?'

'They were wonderful.'

'I'm glad to hear it. I couldn't stand them. I chewed my way through two pipes on that one to Spain.'

The following morning my mother gave us a packed lunch. 'Take the children to see the Bayeux Tapestry,' she said.

'I wouldn't bother,' said my father.

'Don't listen to him,' said my mother.

They had been some years before and my father went around it in ten minutes. He was so quick the museum staff gave him a free coffee at the end. The curator came out of his office and shook his hand. When my mother emerged two hours later he had been round town and read every restaurant menu: '*Porc à la sauce d'haricots noirs, F16,00.*'

We piled into the van and said our goodbyes. My father handed me a brown paper package through the window: 'For use in an emergency; keep it somewhere cool.'

The ferry ploughed down the Solent on a sunny and breezy August morning, yachts scampering out of its way. Down below the camper van had been parked up among the caravans. I ignored the driver in front and he ignored me. We both felt superior to each other.

When the boat docked I imagined the caravans would take the autoroute heading south, while we would head along the Brittany coast and find a lonely camp site looking over the sea, and spend the evening eating *moules* and *frites* in some beach bistro.

It didn't work out like that. The road was like a caravan club rally and every camp site we stopped at was full. Just before dark we found a place that squashed us in next to a couple from Swansea who had won their caravan in a raffle. He wasn't happy though. 'This is a Buccaneer Caravel, single axle. I really wanted to win the Cotswold Celeste.'

He looked at our camper. 'How do you find it?'

'It's good,' I said. 'Very good.'

'You'll have a caravan one day.'

I found the best way to cope was to drink red wine.

The boys didn't care, of course. They loved being on a caravan site. There was ping pong, games of football, a splash pool. 'You're being a grumpy old Brit,' said Catherine and flung a Frisbee at me.

It's just one night, I told myself. Tomorrow we'll find the perfect spot. But the next day was the weekend and even busier. Apparently, the French were interested in the eclipse as well. It was also right in the middle of the French holiday period, and most of Paris had come north: 'for the cooler weather,' said one camper.

Cooler weather is what they got. And rain. On day two some very familiar British-style drizzle settled over the coast. On day three there was thunder. By day four our windscreen wipers were screaming in pain as they passed across the window.

At least the beaches were empty. Our trip to North Wales had prepared us well for this. Alone we went out onto *la plage* in our anoraks. We built castles with wet sand and, since we were in France, played French cricket. 'Why is it called French cricket?' said Catherine.

'Because it's a watered-down version requiring no skill or thought.'

'So it's another way to insult the French.'

'They call us Rosbifs.'

'You call them Frogs.'

'*Le banter*, that's all.'

When a downpour came we ran back into the van and built up a fug. 'This is fun,' said Francis.

And it was fun, thanks largely to that great invention, the audiobook. We all sat behind fogged-up windows captivated by *Northern Lights*. We may have been stuck on the wet coast of Brittany, but in our heads we were journeying to Svalbard with young Lyra, the evil Mrs Coulter and the armoured bears. It was hard to leave the van at times. We had to ration listening time to make sure the story lasted the week.

One evening we limped into a vast camp site near Saint-Quay-Portrieux. The scene that met us was desperate. It was like Glastonbury except there wasn't any music, just fields of tents and caravans, spread over a series of hillsides. With the mud and the rain and all the canvas, it looked as though some terrible disaster had happened and everyone had moved out to this shanty town.

It was, however, a perfect place to study the French on holiday. All life was here. A bread van came round at 6am, a charcuterie van mid-morning. You got your wine from a tap in the camp-site reception. I'll never forget the sight of a glamorous woman in a dressing gown and high heels, striding elegantly along the main thoroughfare, carefully avoiding the puddles, clutching a toilet roll as she headed for *le bloc sanitaire*.

'Did you see that?' I said to Catherine.

'So?'

'Well... it's just...'

'You're turning into your father.'

No I wasn't.

That night we played poker in French. *Le hold'em de Texas*. I bet the van on my hand and lost it to Francis.

'Well son, you now own a 1981 VW Transporter camper van. How does it feel?'

'I'll swap it for a can of beer.'

'Get out of here.'

The next day, with the eclipse just 48 hours away, we headed east to try to escape the rain. The windscreen wipers screeched all the way to Bayeux.

In an effort to prove that I wasn't turning into my father I spent four hours going round the Bayeux Tapestry. The others had to drag me out. 'That was fantastic. Highlight of the holiday. It even featured Halley's Comet, did you see that? If they'd made it in 1999 they'd have put the eclipse in.'

'I reckon William was lucky,' said Francis.

'Why lucky?'

'That arrow went right through the eye slit in Harold's helmet. A lucky shot. The guy who fired it didn't say, "This one is going to get him right in the eye." He couldn't have done it again in a hundred goes.'

We headed on to Arromanches, a pretty Normandy seaside town notable for two things: the off-shore wreck of the Mulberry harbour that the D-Day invasion force assembled, and a crazy golf course where we spent most of our remaining holiday.

The camp site resembled another refugee camp with eclipse pilgrims from all over Europe, caravans and one-man tents pitched next door to each other. The tent next to us played non-stop techno music.

I'd become anaesthetized to it all by now. We joined the crowd wandering round town in the drizzle. I could hear a tinnitus of windscreen wipers in my head.

'You're looking at the menus,' said Catherine.

'No I'm not.'

'Yes you are. I saw you.'

'I was just looking…in restaurant windows.'

I bought postcards and wrote tragic messages.

'Why write such depressing cards?'

'I learnt a long time ago that people prefer to get miserable postcards. They want to hear about flooded camp sites and stomach bugs.'

'We don't have stomach bugs.'

She spoke too soon. We played our fourth crazy golf game of the day and Daniel vomited right across hole number three, which was a Camembert with a slice missing and a hole in it.

We went back to the van and put him to bed. Next door to us two GB motorcyclists had arrived and found room to pitch a tent. One said to me, 'I'd love to have a camper van.'

Part of me wanted to recognize how lucky we were, and part of me wanted to swap it for his bike.

The stomach bug passed quickly. We played poker again that night. This time I bet our house on my hand and again lost it to Francis. 'How does it feel to be a property owner aged ten?'

'I'll swap it for a glass of wine.'

'Get out of here.'

The day of the eclipse dawned, wet and cloudy. At least it was wet and cloudy in Cornwall as well. We decided to drive inland to try to escape the coastal mist, and we found ourselves at a little war cemetery.

'Oh no,' said Catherine. 'We haven't got any special glasses.'

'We're going to go blind!' said Daniel.

'I'm not going to look,' said Francis.

'It's all right,' I said. 'We're lucky enough to have a cloudy day so we won't see it.'

We wandered round the graves to discover it was a German war cemetery. With all the museums documenting the landings of the Allied troops, it was easy to forget that there were two sides on D-Day. But for the war many of these soldiers would have still been alive to witness the rather odd sensation of a cloudy eclipse.

It was an understated sort of experience, but none the less moving. The day turned to evening. The birds stopped singing. The gravestones darkened. We sat on a low wall, wrapped in the kind of solemnity that only a cemetery can create. A peacefulness descended and an unearthly quiet. We held hands and I had never felt closer as a family. After a few minutes the light began to brighten, the birds started to sing once more, and the dark grey sky returned to its more familiar leaden.

'Let's go and have a game of crazy golf,' said Daniel.

'Good idea.'

We played crazy golf all afternoon in the coastal mist. As Francis scored a birdie off the hole where you had to knock the ball through the front door of a lighthouse, he said, 'This has been a great holiday.'

I felt like crying. There was only one thing for it. I left them to get an ice cream and went back to the van and opened the package my father had given me before we left. It was a packet of bacon of course. I'd known it would be and had been determined to resist, but it had been an emotional kind of day.

I made myself a bacon sandwich. Noses lifted and twitched around the camp site. The techno music had stopped for once and I could hear a Mendelssohn violin concerto coming from the caravan next door.

And then the sun came out.

Chapter 22

Road Rage

Everyone in the queue was angry.

Everyone must have been driving around for some time, looking for a filling station that had fuel left, and now we were pushing and shoving our way to the pumps. A woman in a Toyota tried to edge in front of me. I moved forward to block her off; I didn't even look at her.

That was when I first saw the white van. It was nudging up to vehicles, trying to make them give way, as if it had priority. Someone honked their horn. It could have been anyone. Everyone was angry.

Cars made people angry. If it wasn't traffic jams it was parking, or road works or bus lanes or speed cameras, and now fuel protests which had blockaded oil refineries around the country. Some drivers supported the blockades, others railed against them. Wherever you stood you were short of petrol. There was panic buying of course, there always was. But this time it felt different. There was the smell of fear as well as fuel on the garage forecourt. Drivers looked as though they would kill for petrol.

I inched forward. Two drivers ahead were arguing. One was waving the pump in his hand to make a point. His wife was trying to calm him down.

The white van had tucked in behind me now, right on my bumper. The driver was shaking his head in annoyance. You could see him mouthing: 'Come on, for God's sake.'

'Everyone's in a hurry,' I said, safe in the shell of my vehicle. I checked the time. I wanted to get on the motorway by four o'clock, miss the rush hour. 'Come on!'

My turn finally came. I filled up and hurried to the pay station and there was another queue. Some guy in front buying coffee. For God's sake! Then there was a queue to get out of the station onto Upper Street, which in turn was one big jam. The white van was behind me again, still trying to shove his way through. Well he wasn't pushing me out of the way. I edged out into the traffic, a car stopped to let me in. But there was the white van trying to push in front of me. I sat firm. He leant on his horn; he was inches away from me. I looked up and he was mouthing away. I shook my head and swore. 'I've had a hard day too, mate.'

I left him behind at the station and headed north towards Highbury Corner. If I got to the motorway in good time I could be home by seven as long as those road works near Luton weren't too bad. I switched on the radio for traffic news. It was all phone-in shows, rants about the fuel protests. A lorry driver said, 'More than 50 per cent of my petrol bill is tax! It just makes me so angry, Brian.'

I glanced in the mirror and got a shock when I saw the white van again. He was three vehicles back, but as I looked he pulled out and overtook two cars then pushed his way back in. 'Menace,' I muttered.

A government spokesman commented, 'The truth is, in real terms, the price of petrol in 2000 is less than it was in 1980. Fuel has gone up far less than beer or even clothing. All this protesting really makes me quite cross. Angry, even.'

Suddenly my rear-view mirror was all white. The van was right on my back, the driver and his mate grinning down at me. I tried to pull over to let him pass, but he stayed on my tail. Far too close. I felt myself stiffen, sit upright. Two words came to mind: road rage.

There were traffic lights ahead, but I didn't want to stop. I had central locking, but how did I switch that on from the inside? I glanced down at the door handles and looked up just in time to avoid rear-ending the car in front.

Behind me the van screeched as the driver slammed on his brakes, then he leant on his horn again.

At Highbury Corner there were three exits; I was going straight over up the Holloway Road. There was a good chance he'd head off down the Balls Pond Road. But no, he followed me, tailgating me.

I was overreacting. Road rage was just a newspaper term. And yet whenever they wrote about an incident it sounded like an awful experience. Wasn't a driver recently imprisoned for sinking a knife into someone who hadn't let him into traffic? I moved into the outside lane; the van did the same.

I could feel my pulse now. Maybe I'd turn off and see if he followed, but I was reluctant to leave the main road. I could end up getting lost and maybe cornered. I was better off in the full gaze of witnesses.

We moved up towards Archway. Another chance for him to turn off, but he followed me on up the Archway Road. Maybe at the next lights or crossing we came to I'd just get out and knock on his window and apologize: 'I'm sorry if I cut you up back there, it was a momentary aberration. Quite out of character. I need to get back home up to Derbyshire by seven o'clock. It's my son's birthday. Do you have children?'

At Highgate Station a car was edging out of a side road trying to join the traffic. I slowed and let him in, just to show that was how I normally behaved. But all I got was another blare on the horn, and a flash of lights this time. Why did people behave like this just because they were behind a wheel? What made a motorist think he had licence to go round honking at other drivers, giving the finger or winding down windows and shouting? Now that bad behaviour on the road was diagnosed as road rage, now it had its own terminology, drivers thought it was acceptable. It was a medical condition they were helpless to control, like attention deficit disorder. When an angry driver got out of his car and pointed his finger in your face and called you a bastard, you were supposed to be understanding: 'Poor man, he suffers from road rage.'

At the next roundabout were the first signs for the M1. We exited onto the dual carriageway and I moved into the left-hand lane, giving him the chance to overtake, but he tucked in behind me.

I tried to relax. I was being alarmist. This was nothing to get concerned about. I had no proof he was even following me. There was probably some perfectly reasonable explanation. Maybe he was flashing to try and tell me something, like my door was unlocked; or maybe I'd left my credit card at the petrol station. He was following me to give it back. I checked my wallet. My credit card was safely put away.

I turned onto the North Circular. So did he. I tried to ignore him. I changed radio stations. A news report said three-quarters of petrol stations were without fuel. The NHS was cancelling operations because staff couldn't get to work. And yet drivers in north London were wandering about using their precious fuel looking for a filling station that was open so they could panic buy. There was a petrol shortage and the oil companies were making more money than ever.

Past Brent Cross. Soon we would come to the start of the M1. Maybe there'd be a hitchhiker I could pick up, like there always used to be. Preferably a big one, or even two, who would defend me. But it was unlikely. I couldn't remember the last time I'd seen a hitchhiker. People didn't want to share their car-space any more. Drivers preferred isolation; a trip in the car was a chance to be alone. That was why car pools had never caught on in Britain. As MP Steven Norris tactfully put it when explaining why people chose their car over public transport, 'you don't have to put up with dreadful human beings sitting alongside you.'

No hitchhikers. He followed me up the motorway.

I put my foot down. I pulled out into the middle lane and hit the floor. The van did the same. The old Subaru wasn't the car it once was. Actually it was never the car it once was. It could hardly get up the hill out of our valley. It was many years since it had gone 70mph. The white van could easily keep up. The driver was laughing at me and now his white van was laughing at my Subaru.

We passed Scratchwood services. A man in Shropshire came on the radio and said thieves had siphoned petrol from five cars in his street last night. What was going on? How had we become so dependent on petrol? There was going to be civil war because we couldn't do the supermarket run. The man in Shropshire said, 'It's not going to happen again. Me and the neighbours will be waiting for them tonight.'

I couldn't keep running away. I had to take action. If the white van was still behind me at junction 5 I was going to come off, and if he followed me I'd turn into the first lay-by I saw and confront him. I wasn't being bullied any more.

It was time to be brave.

We reached junction 5 and signs for Watford. I moved into the left-hand lane. So did the van. I indicated to come off. So did the van. We moved slowly up the slip-road, took the first exit and cruised down the dual carriageway. I phoned home. I wanted to tell them I loved them. I got the answer machine.

Adrenalin was pumping through me. I knew what I was going to say to him. I was going to be calm and diplomatic. 'Listen. I'm sorry if I didn't let you into the traffic, but does that really give you the right to follow me and stab me…?' Maybe I'd just offer him money.

There was a filling station ahead. I would have pulled in there but a *No Fuel* sign blocked the entrance. Further on I saw a Little Chef. There were a number of cars outside. Some people. Witnesses. 'Right, buddy,' I said. 'This is it.'

I swung off the dual carriageway and into the car park. When I looked behind the van had gone. I saw it disappear down the road, the words *Plasterers* and *Watford* on the side.

In the café I ordered tea. When I tried to open the milk it spurted all over me I was shaking so. I swore under my breath. The people at the table opposite looked wary.

There was a TV on, a news report showing scenes from the road block outside Milford Haven Refinery. A banner read *Go Truck Yourself Gordon Brown*. COBRA, the government's crisis intervention team, was meeting in Whitehall. A farmer who was in the blockade with his tractor said, 'We're paying the highest fuel prices in the western world. Mr Blair needs to know that farmers are angry.'

I wasn't entirely sure why, but I didn't feel any sympathy for the fuel protesters. Part of this was because the rise in fuel prices didn't affect me, or at least I had my own way of dealing with it. I only ever put £40 worth of petrol in my tank. This way a fill-up always cost the same no matter what the price of fuel. The fact that I was able to drive less far as the cost increased never bothered me. It was a delusion that worked for me.

But part of it was because it seemed plain that campaigning against the cost of fuel was the wrong battle. While the government might reduce fuel tax because they didn't want this sort of thing to happen again, the oil itself wasn't going to go down in price. Ever. Oil companies had us over their own barrels, and although cars may be the last things we'd want to give up, the day would come when the cost of motoring would simply be beyond most people.

Everyone agreed there was a finite amount of oil in the world. We could either ration it fairly between everyone, or price it realistically as a luxury item, like gold. More importantly, instead of fighting for tax cuts we needed to develop alternatives to oil that were sustainable.

Unfortunately, I didn't feel man enough to write that on a placard and go and wave it in front of all the angry truckers and farmers outside Ellesmere Port.

The TV report ended with the news that a convoy of protesting lorry drivers was moving at slow speed up the M1 causing delays from Northampton to Nottingham.

I growled in frustration. The people at the table opposite buttoned their coats and asked for the bill. I went back to my car and swore out loud. I wasn't going to get home before midnight.

I drove off through the car park, and when a car reversed out, causing me to brake, I leant on my horn and glared at him. Mr Angry.

Chapter 23

Roadie

The camper van's days were numbered. Little things like opening the sliding door and seeing it just keep sliding, ending up with a crash on the ground. Part of the runner had rusted away. I managed to refit it, but it had to be opened with a special pull, push and tug technique that only I knew.

The door was merely the latest casualty of rust. Elsewhere the gutters had gone, the wheel arches looked diseased, the roof was rusting from the inside out. I was no expert, but the prognosis looked poor.

We couldn't complain. We'd had good value from the van, good times. If ever there was a vehicle I was going to get sentimental over this was the one. We had taken it round Scotland and Wales, to the beaches of Cornwall and Norfolk. We went abroad a number of times to France and along the Spanish north coast. We all went to the Edinburgh Festival in it and camped on the edge of town. We spent a wedding anniversary in it in the New Forest.

We used it until the boys simply grew too big. Their legs stuck out over the edge of the top bunk. The engine was still able but it sighed a lot and became too risky to take on long trips. I wondered if I should restore it myself – since we'd had it the Transporter series had become collectable – but I laughed at the idea. It needed someone with skills to take it on as a project.

I was on the verge of selling it. But then, against all the odds, it reinvented itself one last time. It entered the world of rock 'n' roll.

One of the last weekend trips we took in the van was to the Rhythm and Blues Festival in Colne in Lancashire. The boys both played guitars; they had pictures of Hendrix on their wall; Daniel's 14th birthday cake was in the shape of a Fender Strat. They were desperate to be in a band.

Lots of the acts at Colne were from the sixties, so the adults were happy too. We saw The Animals, Dave Edmunds, Wilko Johnson. Even Jerry Lee Lewis's sister played. But there was one band that made a bigger impression on me than all of these.

They were in the corner of a pub without so much as a stage, a band of four hairy teenagers, playing so loudly the glasses around the bar rattled in time. But there was a fifth member, an older man, bald and with a belly. His job was to hurry between the van which you could see parked just outside and the band, bringing in equipment as it was needed, then crawling around between legs and plugging things in. For some reason I identified with this man. When the crowd cheered at the end, I cheered for him. When the crowd called 'Encore' – by which time the band was supping pints and the older man was having a cup of tea from a flask (I assumed because he was driving) – I shouted 'Encore' for him. When the lead singer stepped up to the mic again, waving to his fans while at the same time gesticulating to the old boy for a different guitar, I knew what their relationship was: father and son.

On the way home, the boys played the CDs they had bought. By the time we got back they had decided they were going to form their own band. 'I want to be drummer,' said Daniel.

'No, *I* want to be drummer,' said Francis.

In the end neither of them were drummer because they didn't have any drums. One played keyboards and the other played guitar. They recruited a bass player and a drummer with his own kit. There was, however, one position still vacant.

'So how are you going to get to gigs and things?' I asked Daniel.

'We haven't got a gig.'

'But when you do?'

'I don't know.'

'You're going to need transport for all the equipment.'

'Guess so.'

'I can drive you in the van.'

'If you like.'

'I'd be sort of road manager.'

'If you want.'

Yes!! I was in a band.

The role of road manager in the history of rock 'n' roll is an unsung one, and yet, I would say, it's fundamental to any success.

No matter how famous a band gets it will, at some point, have depended on someone with wheels to get them to and from gigs. Neil Aspinall is the best-known road manager simply because he drove for the best-known band. All through the early years of The Beatles he ferried them and their gear around in his Comma van. It was Neil Aspinall who drove the young hopefuls down the new M1 to London on New Year's Eve 1961 for their first recording at Decca. He got badly lost and they took ten hours to get there. The band didn't perform any better at their audition and they came away empty-handed.

My band wasn't quite at the recording contract stage yet. We weren't even at the gig stage. The boys spent all their rehearsal time trying to think of a name.

'How about The Sharks?' I said. They ignored me.

'How about The Rockhards?' said Eddie the bass player.

'I want to be called The Misery-guts,' said Jake the drummer.

'How about The Barracudas?' I said.

'What is with it you and fish?' said Francis.

They got their first gig, a friend's 16th birthday party. I tried to contain my excitement. The fact that the gig was only 200 yards away, and a roadie wasn't really necessary, made no difference. Wembley Arena or the local village hall, the gear had to get there.

I loaded up the van then went to pick up the drummer. 'Don't open the sliding doo...!' Too late, the door hit the ground like a crash of cymbals.

The old van sagged under the weight of the amps, but we made it round the corner to the hall and set up. They still hadn't thought of a name for themselves. 'How about The Ocelots?' said the drummer.

'The Four-eyed Owls,' said Francis.

They were going through a wildlife phase.

'The Badgers.'

'The Dinosaurs.'

'How about The Piranhas?' I said.

'What's a piranha?'

'Creature with razor sharp teeth that tears the flesh off prey.'

This appealed. The gig was a success and the name stuck.

'I see great things for The Piranhas,' I said to Catherine after we'd safely made the journey back from the village hall without the door coming off again. 'Did you know, on The Beatles' first tour of America, Neil Aspinall actually stood in for George Harrison for a photo shoot when George had a temperature of 102?'

'That's not going to happen to you though, is it?'

'He even got to play tambourine on "Within You and Without You" on *Sgt Pepper*.'

'I think you should stick to what you're good at.'

'I'm good at tambourine.'

'Driving the van.'

Other birthday party gigs followed. They played at a dance in a golf club. They got a gig at the opening of an extension to a DIY store managed by the bass player's dad, on the condition they didn't play too loud.

As they got more bookings they needed more gear: a mixing table, some lights, speakers. Throughout the summer the van did the leg work while the kids took the glory. It may have laboured up some hills, but with Green Day and Limp Bizkit coming through the one speaker that worked, you could smell the excitement. Four boys who really thought they were heading for the big time.

Things started to get serious when they played a local talent show and won. They beat a 12-year-old violinist and a juggling tap-dancer. It was an unforgettable night. Mainly because the whole place was hopping, but also because on the way home the van's gear lever came off in my hand.

Normally if the van developed a problem I just ignored it and eventually it went away. The engine would go through periods of not wanting to start; the temperature gauge would soar to boiling; I once wound down the window and couldn't get it up again. All these issues somehow corrected themselves. A gear lever coming off was different though. It wasn't going to grow a new one or anything. I managed to drive it home in third and the next day got it to the garage. It was due for its MOT anyway. When I went to pick it up the mechanic said, 'I thought you were going to get rid of this.'

'It's rediscovering its youth.'

He nodded. 'It's been an interesting MOT. Never seen so much flora and fauna on a vehicle. There's a range of different lichens growing around the windows, and some silverfish nesting in the gear housing.'

'It's parked under a tree.'

'And there's a mouse living in there somewhere.'

'Right.'

'First time I've written "Buy a mousetrap" in the Advisory Items column.'

After the talent show win, The Piranhas made a recording and entered a nationwide competition. They were told they had been chosen out of thousands to appear in Manchester in a regional final, A Battle of the Bands. 'The winner,' read out Daniel, 'gets to professionally record a CD and play at the grand final in the O2 Arena.'

They practised every spare minute they had. They wrote their own song. They dumped the name The Piranhas when they discovered it referred to fish, and renamed themselves The Revolutionaries. They grew in confidence. I was the only anxious one. I knew the van could cope driving to gigs locally, but Manchester was a distance, and, if they got through and were invited to London, well, it wouldn't make it. We would have to leave it at home and hire a vehicle, which didn't seem fair. It would have been like The Beatles sacking Pete Best just before they got famous – a sour episode in their history which appalled my mentor Neil Aspinall at the time, not least because he was having an affair with Pete Best's mum.

I worked on the van as the boys worked on their music. Emails came telling them that the judges were looking for more than musical ability and presentation. A fan base was just as important; they needed to show they had a following.

'They're 16. How are they going to have a fan base?'

'We'll create a fan base,' said Catherine.

All the parents bought tickets and co-opted friends and relatives. We invited the grandparents up. We'd show them what a fan base was.

'Good journey?' I asked my father when he arrived.

'Not bad. M5, M6.'

Times had changed. In the past when you asked him if he'd had a good journey he'd sit you down and give a 20-minute travelogue, something like: 'Not bad, took the A350 to Chippenham and then picked up the A46, delightful little road through the Cotswolds, shame about the road works near Stow-on-the-Wold. Had a coffee break near Kidderminster...' and so on. But now every long journey was a quick drive to the motorway and that was the end of it. M5, M6 it was, and would be forever.

There was one note of interest though. Somehow they'd ended up on the M6 toll road. 'Your mother was navigating. Cost £6 just to use the bloody motorway. If I want to pay for roads I can go to France thank you very much. £6! I refused to pay.'

'What happened?'

'Your mother coughed up.'

They'd driven in the new Rover. After 50 years he'd finally got one. 'It's made in Japan of course, like all the good cars these days.'

The big day arrived. I cleaned the van, not too roughly – bits fell off if you brushed it too hard. I tried to wipe off all evidence of mould from around the edges. I cleared the roof of hawthorn blossom. We put drinks and a cake in the fridge just in case they won.

The boys spent a long time getting ready. There was more oil on their hair than in my engine. We loaded the gear and set off in convoy: the band up front, the fan base following. I gave the van a good run at the hill and it made it with a bit of a splutter. It was making an effort.

The boys were unusually quiet on the way. Only once did Eddie the drummer speak: 'I hate the name The Revolutionaries.'

When we got there it was clear that this was a step up. The venue was a big club somewhere in the Manchester suburbs and as soon as we entered the car park I had a bad feeling. Other bands had arrived in customized SUVs or Transit vans with their name splashed along the side. There were coaches full of fans. There were a lot of teenage girls screaming and running round asking for autographs.

The Revolutionaries tried to remain cool, but I could tell they were terrified. Two girls ran up to them and asked what band they were. Francis said, 'The Revolutionaries.'

'The Revolutionaries!' they shrieked.

'Yeah, but we can't stand the name,' said the drummer.

The girls looked at the van. 'Is this your band bus?'

They all said no.

'Can we have your autograph?'

They all said no.

We unloaded the gear and headed inside. But I was stopped at the stage door by security. 'Band members only.'

'I'm road manager,' I protested.

They laughed, and I was sent round the front to buy a ticket. But it was sold out. The place was packed, mostly with grandparents.

I'd heard them play so many times I wasn't going to cause a fuss. I went back to the van, made a cup of tea and sat with the newspaper. A limo pulled up and four teenage boys dressed in black jumped out. Behind came the parents in the family Vauxhall.

A voice said, 'We used to have one like this.' A man in his fifties wearing a T-shirt that read *Like Thunder,* and underneath, *Crew,* was eyeing up the van. 'A VW camper with a pop top, just like this, same colour even. We went all over in it.'

I gave him a cup of tea. He said, 'I see your gutters are going.'

'It's parked under a tree.'

'Has your door come off yet?'

'Yes.'

'Tell me about it.' He shook his head, in that hopeless way. 'That's why we decided to buy the minibus and trailer.'

He looked across the car park to his dark blue van with shaded windows and a trailer attached that had *Like Thunder* written in flames along the side.

'Like Thunder. Good name,' I said.

'Yeah. They're loud and frightening. They're going places. They want me to buy a Winnebago. What's your lot called?'

'The Revolutionaries.'

'They won't like that. Sounds political. They don't like anything political.'

He'd been doing this with his son's band for a couple of years. Like Thunder had played at many regional finals, but never won.

'All the family's come. We bought tickets for the next door neighbours this time.'

I was beginning to understand. That's why the place was filled with older people rather than teenagers. It was a racket. The organizers knew that parents and family would go anywhere to see their children perform. You could charge them twenty quid a ticket with no complaints. The more heats you had the more money you made. It wasn't about the music, it was about the size of the crowd you brought along, and how loud they were.

My friend said, 'I told them: you get to the O2 and I'll buy a Winnebago then.'

The boys came out, jumping up in the air and high-fiving each other. They hadn't won, they weren't going to the O2. 'But guess what? We've been asked to go to a third place final in Birmingham.'

'What's the prize?'

'There isn't a prize,' said Daniel. 'It's another opportunity to build up our fan base.'

We had the black forest gateau. 'What did you think?' I asked my father.

He said, 'I think your boys have got talent.'

'Good.'

'But not for music.'

The Birmingham gig was a month away. But things changed in that time. The van door came off again and this time I couldn't put it back. I fixed a piece of tarpaulin over the opening. No one was going to Birmingham in this.

But the boys also began to lose interest. Francis said, 'One of the other bands loosened my strings, so my guitar was out of tune.'

'They said we were crap,' said Daniel.

'It's tough at the top,' I said.

When they were offered a gig at a Young Farmers social on the same night as Birmingham, they decided to take it. 'Why?' I asked.

'They're paying us £5 each.'

'And the road manager?'

'They didn't say anything about the road manager.'

Well, if I wasn't getting a cut they could arrange their own transport.

I sold the van shortly afterwards. The fact that it had a tarpaulin instead of a door didn't seem to put off prospective buyers.

It was years since I'd sold a vehicle, and I imagined I'd be posting the details off to newspapers and fielding phone calls, but of course the internet was made for selling anything collectible. I advertised on the local Gumtree website with photos, and within hours I had a list of people wanting to come and view it. One man phoned from his car as he was driving down the Welsh coast. When I told him I'd had lots of interest, he turned round and came that night.

I parked it under the nearest street light, but essentially he agreed to buy it in the dark. He slapped a deposit in my hand. I immediately wondered if I was letting go of something I didn't know the value of, but all I had to do was look at the rust on the wheel arches and realize it needed to belong to someone who would look after it.

He came with the rest of the money later in the week. We shook hands and he headed off up the hill out of the valley. I watched through binoculars as he climbed the switchback.

I had this daydream that if I ever saw the van again it would be restored to its prime, rust free, a nice paint job, no weeds growing in the window frames, proudly motoring down through France with another family on board.

But for now I just wanted to make sure it made it out of the valley one last time. Once it was over the ridge it was his responsibility, not mine.

Chapter 24

The Golden Age of Motoring

'So I gave Francis a driving lesson the other day. He sat in the car, in the Fiesta – did I tell you we bought a Fiesta? – we've still got the Subaru, but this is a little runaround, perfect to learn to drive in. You know how our cars are always beat up and full of dents? Well, that's not going to happen with this one, because it was like that when we bought it. Anyway, he was really nervous, but not half as nervous as me. I sat there thinking, "This boy was only born a few years ago; he's only just out of short pants and here he is driving a car. I must be mad. I've seen him play Formula 1 on PlayStation – he's lethal."'

I was speaking to my father, but he couldn't answer back. He was very ill, in a coma in fact. He'd recently had the latest in a series of strokes and now it was just a matter of time.

'I tried to be calm. But as soon as he started the engine my foot lunged for the imaginary brake pedal. It was a disaster. He actually managed to have an accident before we left the driveway. It's true. He hit the Subaru.'

The doctors said we should keep talking to him. He may be in a coma but there was a good chance he could still hear. So we took it in turns to sit and chat. This was all right for ten minutes, 15 perhaps, but after that one-way conversations could become a struggle.

'Francis says I screamed at him and used language he'd never heard before, even in the football team. I can't believe that's true.

'I remember you teaching me to drive; you were very calm; you wore your cravat and a flat cap. Doesn't seem that long ago. Anyway, his mother's taking him out while I'm down here. Probably for the best.'

The conversation always worked its way round to cars. They were still his biggest interest, along with bacon. He'd had a blood pressure problem for ages. Knowing how much he liked to check pressures we bought him a gauge so he could test himself at home. It gave him hours of fun. If you went to see him he tested your blood pressure as well. He tested the dog. 'That dog needs medication.'

'So, soon he'll be driving; he's just got to pass his test. But they've no idea, these kids. Can't change a wheel. Wouldn't know how to check a battery. 'Course, you don't need to check a battery any more do you? They're all sealed. They've no interest in road maps or road numbers either. They've no idea where anywhere is. They say, "Put it into the satnav."'

A silence, just the gentle hum of air conditioning. The distant rattle of a trolley.

'Tell you what I saw on the drive down: one of those trucks with a sign on the back that says *How am I driving?* Funny how those vehicles are always the ones that go tearing round the place. But does anyone ever phone up and say how they're driving? No, they never do.

'You used to though, didn't you? You used to stop at the next service station and find a pay phone and give a detailed account of what you thought of their driver: "Generally pretty good, although I noticed a tendency to brake too hard when approaching traffic lights. Instead of a smooth and gradual deceleration there was too much of this 'slamming on the anchors' business. And he threw a cigarette end out of the window which brought his overall score down. Six out of ten.'"

Outside in the car park the Rover pulled up. My mother had picked up my brother from the station. It was her car now. There was a cushion on the driver's seat, and Classic FM on the radio instead of his beloved Radio 2.

'Cones Hotline, that was another of your favourites wasn't it? Remember that one – John Major's idea. That phone number they put on road works signs, and drivers phoned up and complained.

'Or you did anyway. You were the only person I ever knew who phoned the Cones Hotline. They probably knew you down at the control centre.

'I think they closed it because drunks were calling in to order ice creams.'

My brother came in. When you were on your own with my father you could say what you liked. When there were two of you it should have been easier, but in fact it was harder. You couldn't just talk to the other person, you had to include the coma patient as well.

My brother had the same idea as I did. He said, 'I was trying to make a list on the way down of all the cars you've ever owned. There was the Ford Anglia to start with.'

'It was a Ford Pop,' I said.

'It was an Anglia. It looked like a box on wheels.'

'It was a Ford Pop, looked just like the Anglia.'

'That's because it was an Anglia. I remember the little insignia on the back.'

We weren't going to have an argument in front of our comatose father were we?

'Next was the Hillman,' said Andrew.

'That's right. We had two Hillmans.'

'Two Hillmans, the first one was blue and grey.'

'It was cream and mauve.'

'No, the second was cream and mauve.'

How could two memories differ so?

'Then came the Morris Oxford,' said Andrew.

'That was a great car.'

'Then the Austin 1800.'

'It was a Morris 1800.'

Maybe my father was enjoying this conversation. Or maybe he wanted us to stop squabbling and wave a bacon sandwich under his nose. We kept going for an hour, rearranging the list: the 1800s, the two Granadas, the Capri. Then the Rover years: the mustard coloured one, the plum, the silver grey. We drew up the definitive list of the cars of Bryan Harold Wallington. And left it propped up by his bedside.

'One thing I've always wondered,' I said, addressing my father, 'was why you always made a note of the mileage before you went anywhere.'

We waited for him to respond. After a respectful pause Andrew said, 'It's obvious why.'

'Why?'

'Because then you know how far it is.'

'How far what is?'

'Where you've been...I do it myself.'

Back home I gave Francis another driving lesson. This time I tried to be more relaxed. I wore dark glasses and shorts and slouched in the seat. 'Off you go,' I said. 'Just drive naturally, it doesn't matter if you hit anything.'

A tractor came straight for us. I tried not to flinch. I sat gripping the seat with my buttocks. Further on he stalled at some traffic lights and started to panic. 'Nothing to worry about,' I said as a cement lorry towered over us.

He tried reversing round a corner and ended up on the pavement. His three-point turn was a six-pointer. 'Happens to all of us,' I said.

As we stopped at a busy junction he looked puzzled. 'What's the matter?' I asked.

'Why's Grandpa dying?'

This really wasn't the time.

'Why's he dying?'

There was a queue of cars behind us. Someone tooted.

Francis tried to set off, but stalled again. The car behind overtook. I said. 'There are lots of reasons why Grandpa's dying. But mainly because...he's just reached the end of the road. That and too many bacon sandwiches.'

We managed to get home unscathed. 'Okay. Now let's try some hand signals.'

'What are hand signals?'

'Hand signals. For slowing down, turning left and right.'

'You don't have to learn hand signals any more.'

He showed me the syllabus. It was true. How could hand signals no longer be important? I said, 'You mean, if someone in front of you sticks their hand out of the window and waves it up and down you don't know what it means?'

'No.'

This was the first indication I had that I was approaching old age. I said, 'Do you know that your grandfather never took a driving test? He learnt during...'

'...World War II. Yes, you've told me.'

'Have I?'

'Many times.'

That was the second indication.

Hand signals may no longer have been on the test, but learners did need to know how to check oil, water and brake fluid. Just the sort of thing my father would have loved to have taught his grandson: the art of fluid level checking.

'Okay,' I stood by Francis in the driveway, oil can at the ready. 'The first thing you need to do is open the bonnet. You know how to do that?'

'No.'

'Oh come on.'

'I don't know!'

'Well get in there and work it out. It's not difficult.'

He fumbled around the dashboard and steering wheel, but couldn't locate a release switch. 'I can't find it.'

'Pretend it's an emergency. You're on Snake Pass and you've run out of oil. You can't possibly drive it any more. You have to find the release button.'

He searched again. 'Still can't find it.'

'Oh come here, let me do it.'

I got in the driving seat. I'd never actually opened the bonnet on the Fiesta before. For all my father's obsession with fluid levels I was utterly negligent. I checked them once every six months, or when the warning light came on, or the brakes got spongy. I fumbled around. I turned the wipers on by mistake. I switched on the hazard lights.

'That's odd. It must be here somewhere.'

'I'll Google it.'

'You're not going to Google "how do I open the bonnet on a Fiesta?"'

I crawled in and looked round under the steering wheel and down the side of the seat. Why would they make it so difficult? I pulled every button I could. But it was no use.

'Right. Well. I think what we'll do is move on to tyres. We'll get the oil checked next time we're at the garage.'

'We can't go anywhere. We're stuck up on Snake Pass. Remember?'

'Oh go and Google it.'

He Googled it. The bonnet release was the huge orange lever under the steering wheel, so huge and so orange neither of us had dared touch it.

My father died within a few weeks. We busied ourselves with the funeral. The undertaker gave us a brochure with all the details. There at the bottom of the page was a list of the different hearses you could choose from. 'Look, you can have a motorbike and side-car hearse,' said my brother.

'You can also get a vintage flat-bed lorry,' said my sister, 'but we're not having one.'

'He didn't like to bring attention to himself,' I said.

'If you're in a hearse you can't help but draw attention to yourself,' said my sister. 'I say we go for the Rolls-Royce.'

This was getting out of hand. My mother had the final say. 'Maybe we should stick with the Mercedes.'

We sat around, waiting, listening to the grandfather clock tick. The traffic on the bypass seemed to be quieter out of respect. My brother said, 'I'm going to prove to you that Hillman was blue and grey.'

He dug out the cine-camera projector and dusted off the screen. There was a box of reels with labels such as *Maypole Dancing 1960, Donkey Derby 1962*. It didn't matter which one we looked at, the family cars always featured. There was my father in his Capri, my mother in her Mini. But then there he was climbing out of a car I'd never seen before. 'What car was that?' I said.

'That was the Morris Minor,' said my mother.

'We never had a Morris Minor.'

'Of course we did. It was before the first Hillman.'

'No.'

'SFX 237.'

'You can remember the licence plate?'

'Of course. I can remember them all. He used to test me on them.'

My brother and I were astonished. A car that neither of us could remember? It didn't seem possible.

'I can't watch any more of these,' I said. I was frightened we might discover a sibling we never knew we had.

'We never found out what colour the Hillman was,' said my brother.

'First or second?' said my mother.

'First.'

'Two-tone brown and cream. HKN 675.'

At 9.30 on the morning of the funeral two Mercedes came to the house: one containing the coffin, the other to transport the family. 'I've never been able to get a car that clean,' I said to the pallbearer. He smiled and nodded. He was used to people making inane comments.

I walked round the hearse as if inspecting it. It was at nervous moments like this that my father would have found it impossible to resist taking the tyre pressure: whip out the old gauge, a quick duck down when no one was looking, unscrew the valve cap and Bob's your uncle. What happened to that tyre pressure gauge anyway?

I asked my mother but she didn't know. It was at the back of my mind throughout the service. It was such an important and ever present part of his wardrobe he might have wanted to be buried with it.

After it was all over I searched through his drawers, among all the motoring paraphernalia: the many driving gloves, old AA gazetteers, the road atlases, the charts he drew up each spring when he and my mother went off on a French motoring trip. He did all the driving, she did all the talking. They were a perfect match really.

I searched in his tallboy and eventually found the tyre pressure gauge in his stud box. I asked my mother if I could keep it.

'Don't tell the others.'

Francis took his driving test later in the summer and failed. 'Almost everyone fails their first test,' I told him. 'There's only one man in our family who didn't fail his first test.'

'Who?'

'Your grandpa.'

'Because he didn't take a test!' We both laughed.

He passed at the second attempt. But then when we tried to put him on the insurance the company wanted £1,200. While he was learning the premium was expensive, but just about affordable. Now he had a full licence the last thing they wanted him doing was driving anywhere, so they priced him off the road.

'What was all that about a driving licence being a passport to independence?' he said.

I could feel something drawing to a close here. My father had convinced me that a driving test was a rite of passage, it would change my life, and he'd been right. I'd said the same thing to my son, but it was no longer true. The huge cost of motoring now meant a driving licence was of little consequence.

His friends were in the same position of course. Very few could afford to run a vehicle – the boys anyway.

'I just discovered girls get cheaper insurance,' Francis protested. 'That's discrimination.'

The reason girls got cheaper insurance was demonstrated pretty quickly, when the only lad in the village who did have his own car went out and totalled it.

Francis and his friends got round their transport difficulties somehow. They bought young person's railcards, or shared taxis back from town. They didn't seem bothered. Driving just didn't have the same allure it once did. Cars were associated with climate change rather than the open road. They still ruled our lives, but they no longer excited.

My father and I had lived through the golden age of motoring. And we'd never known it.

Chapter 25

The End of the Road

I always thought one day I would have a nice car. Nothing particularly flashy, just something solid and well made with a decent engine; comfortable and easy on the eye. A no-compromise car.

This was always going to be hard with children. Our cars quickly became wrecks. The Subaru had always been a fantastic mess, full of rubbish and with so many dents it looked like it had rolled down an embankment. It wasn't just disposable coffee cups you found under the seat, but dinner plates, clothing and animal bones. If anything was lost or you needed some loose change, the first place you looked was in the car. The day we bought it we managed to spill a pint of milk in the footwell, and it had a sour whiff its entire life.

When the children left home I imagined things would change. But no. I went out one morning to find the Subaru's hatchback had been left open all night, a rainy night, and there was an inch of water inside. A box of dog food had become saturated and a biscuity soup swamped the floor. A sock floated by happily. Road atlas pages, CDs and other assorted flotsam lapped at the corners. I knew then that I would only ever have the car I deserved.

After ten years' neglect the Subaru developed a death rattle. We didn't dare take it to the garage. It was like the patient who was too ill to go the doctor. As long as it started and drove we could cope. But then the MOT came round and the mechanic needed an extra sheet of paper to list all the failed items.

'What's it going to cost to get through?'

He shrugged. 'Seven hundred quid.'

'What's the car worth?'

He had a good think and then said, 'It's not worth anything.'

When I told Catherine she said, 'We should buy a Prius like the Radcliffes.'

'I don't want a Prius.'

'We have to think of our carbon footprint.'

'Priuses are too quiet. They give me the creeps.'

The four-wheel drive fad was on the wane. The growing trend was to buy the greenest, most worthy vehicle. The Prius was the brand leader among the hybrids but, as with four-wheel drives, all manufacturers were taking an interest.

'There's a Honda here with solar panels,' said Catherine.

I sighed. The thought of buying a new car used to give me a thrill, but now it was a chore. In the end our choice was made after a visit to a racing drivers' school in Cheshire.

It was a birthday present from my brother, a drive round a race track in an open single seater. We all went down for the day. I was given overalls and a helmet and joined five other novices in a lecture room where an instructor talked very seriously about something called the Racing Line. We were taken round the circuit by a driver in a race car who also kept talking about the Racing Line. We had lunch, during which the conversation was dominated by the Racing Line. In the afternoon our big moment came.

The flag went down and we roared off. Or everyone else did. I found myself uneasy at going anything above a sensible speed. I don't think I broke the 70mph national speed limit once on my five circuits. Cars lapped and overtook me on either side, but I just kept motoring along, quite enjoying myself actually. I thought of the racing drivers of my youth: Stirling Moss, Jim Clark, Jackie Stewart. I thought of Donald Campbell and *Bluebird* taking off in an elegant somersault over Coniston Water, and I knew I was an embarrassment to them all.

I came last of course, by a very long way. The instructor handed out the time sheets afterwards and commented on each one. To most people he said, 'Good line.' With me, he struggled to find the right words. He said, 'You see, driving is all about being an extension of the car.'

And I thought, 'Not any more it isn't.'

On the way home we made a list of the things that we wanted in a new vehicle. It was simple really: we wanted something with low emission and good mpg; we wanted something that didn't break down; and we wanted something for which parts were reasonably priced. If we could find a car that mended its own dents that would be a bonus. We wanted a good music system. And we wanted somewhere you could put milk bottles without them spilling. The one thing I didn't want was a car that needed me to be an extension of it.

With all this in mind we headed to the car supermarket.

It was a cold grey day with banks of fog across the moors. The car supermarket loomed just off the motorway. You couldn't miss it: a huge banner and a parking lot full of shiny, recently valeted vehicles.

We stepped through the automatic doors into the air-conditioned reception. I could smell coffee, hear soft music. I prepared myself for an immediate attack by a sales person, but instead a young woman in heels passed us and said, 'Are you all right there?'

'Fine.'

'Help yourselves to coffee. Have a browse on the computer. I'm here if you want some help.'

This had to be a trick. Instinctively my hand covered my wallet. I backed towards the coffee machine and poured two cups, then we sat down at a computer terminal. There were plenty of staff, but none watching us.

'There must be cameras,' I said. 'They're monitoring us in the control room.'

Catherine entered our details, our requirements and price range. In 0.5833 of a second the computer came back with 20 results, and they were all Ford Focuses.

'What's a Ford Focus?' she said.

I read, 'The Ford Focus is one of the most complete cars on the road today. Well designed, well engineered, well built, well priced. It drives superbly. It's reliable and economic. Nothing has come close to making the Focus anything other than the most easily recommendable car in its class.'

'I think we should buy one,' said Catherine.

'You're so easily persuaded. You always have been. You always buy the first car you're recommended.'

'What do you suggest?'

'I suggest we buy a Ford Focus as well.'

There was a courtesy bus that left every ten minutes, taking customers to the aisle of their choice. 'We'd like to go to the Datsuns,' said one couple to the driver, as if they were asking him to drop them off at the post office. Another couple got out at the Renaults. I gazed out of the window as the bus drove on past the Vauxhalls, the Hondas, the Audis, the Nissans, and I thought how I really didn't like cars much any more. I knew how important they had been in my life, how in every memory there was a car somewhere in the frame, and how intrinsic they had been to the culture of the last 100 years, but now... driving was something I tried to avoid.

We were the last stop, in a corner of the lot, where a whole aisle of Ford Focuses sat glumly.

'How about an estate?' said Catherine.

'Estates are always a good idea.'

'What colour?'

'They're all sort of grey.'

'There's a blue one there.'

'It's a grey kind of blue though, isn't it. How about charcoal?'

'Charcoal is good. Doesn't show the dents.'

We made a note of the number plate. 'Shall we walk or take the bus?'

'I feel like a walk.'

There was no need for a test drive or anything like that. It was like at Tesco: if it didn't work or you didn't like it you brought it back for a refund. A woman named Becky with a 'Negotiator' badge sat us down. The price was £8,500, she said. We offered her £8,000, thinking she would negotiate, but she said, 'Okay £8,000. Do you have something to trade in?'

'We most certainly do. A fine Subaru which has been a sturdy family vehicle for many years, and has a lot more miles in it yet, if someone will simply put it through its MOT.'

'How old.'

'A mere 12 years.'

'We'll knock £60 off the total.'

'It's a deal.'

We went back to pick it up when the paperwork was all done. We said our goodbyes to the Subaru. 'Ah, still smells like an old cheese,' said Catherine.

'Yes, and look, there's that paint stain where a can of yellow emulsion got tipped over, and there's that tear in the seat fabric where the boys used it as a bread board. And look down there, there are 35 pens of assorted colours lodged under the seat.'

We swapped keys. The new car smelt of carpet cleaner and pine air fresheners. We drove away and that was that.

'We need to stop and pick up some milk on the way home,' said Catherine.

When the children were small we once went to a motor museum, and the thing I remember the most about the old cars was the beauty and texture of the paintwork. There was nothing metallic or glossy about it. They were flat, matt colours that looked as though they'd been applied by a good painter and decorator.

And what colours! Beautiful duck egg greens, royal blues, postal reds; and many vehicles in two-tone blues or yellows. I recall a simple Vauxhall Victor in stylish forest green and black. It was all about trying to look different, to stand out in a crowd.

The Ford Focus specializes in not being noticed. I often lose it in car parks among all the other grey cars. We didn't buy it for its style though. We bought it because we wanted something reliable, and you can't fault it for that. Everything works as well as the day it was bought. It's taken all the uncertainty out of running a car.

Only once has it given us a fright. Catherine said, 'There's a red light on the dashboard.'

'What red light?'

'A nice little red light.'

I went and checked. It was a display I'd never seen before. I looked in the manual and it warned that if this particular light ever came on the driver was to stop immediately and call for assistance.

'It's been on for a couple of days,' said Catherine. 'Maybe a week.'

I lifted the bonnet. If there was anything wrong with it there was no clue there. Nothing to unscrew and peer into.

We took it to the garage. 'It's all diagnostics these days,' said the mechanic. 'We'll run it through the computer.'

He ran it through the computer. 'The computer says it needs a new spark plug.'

How thoughtful.

No worries and no surprises. The car never changes. Perhaps it's got a little more grey over the last two years, a little more like all the other cars on the road. I've no idea what the registration number is. The most exciting thing that's happened to me in the Focus was hitting the gatepost. Yes, it was me who gave it its first dent. I sometimes wonder if I did it on purpose just to have some sort of emotional experience in it.

You can't blame a car for being dull though. Cars are like dogs, they say: they reflect the owner, and I suppose I've become a dull driver. I go where the satnav tells me to. I smile for the speed cameras. I pay congestion charges and tolls without thinking. I trust in my airbag. I have a sizeable no claims bonus. I stay tuned to Radio 4, and avoid jams by listening to traffic bulletins.

The Focus starts every morning without fail. It uses next to no oil; the fluid levels never change, nor the tyre pressures. There's something robotic about it. There's no sign of rust of course. Rust is a thing of the past. When we first bought it the man at the car supermarket said, 'This will see you out, this will.'

He laughed and I laughed. But I wondered. When I got home I Googled 'how long does a Ford Focus last?' And there were stories of '150,000 miles and still going strong'. At that rate, and knowing the way we drive cars into the ground, there is indeed a chance this charcoal grey Ford, with no discernible features and no character other than its interminable reliability, will be the last car I ever buy.

The very idea should be depressing. But it isn't. Aged 60, and having had a driving licence for 43 years, I now know it's not about the car. It never has been. It's about where the car takes you. It took a trip to the other side of the world to make this clear.

I was working on a project which required me to travel
out to New Zealand. I was met at Auckland Airport by a
development executive from South Pacific Pictures who
shook my hand, sat me down and gave me some maps.
Then handed me two envelopes.

Inside one was a wad of cash. In the other, a car key.

'Thanks,' I said.

'Have fun,' she replied.

Was I feeling giddy because of the jet lag or because of
what had just happened? I hunted round the airport
parking lot for my hire car, then sat inside and counted the
money, and I thought: you've finally made it.

For the next two weeks I drove around the North
Island, cruising down long and undulating highways,
volcanoes on one side, rugged coastline on the other,
staying in small and sunny towns where you could always
park on the main street.

I was researching a film about a Maori community and
had introductions that took me to the villages. The Maori
were very kind and welcoming, keen to help and include
me in their everyday life. In one village I was invited to
play in the weekly game of bingo. In another I was taken
to a funeral.

I was just wandering about, writing everything down. I
bought some blues CDs and happily cruised the empty
roads, tapping the steering wheel in time. I had no real
destination; I went where people suggested I go.

I ended up in the far north, travelling through the kauri
forests, across inlets on little ferries and on to the Ninety
Mile Beach where I stayed at a remote motel almost on
the sand. The boom of the waves was relentless and the air

tasted of salt. The motel was run by a Maori and his wife, who had red hair from her Scottish ancestry. There was nowhere to get dinner nearby and I was grateful when she asked me to eat with them. She said, 'Do you want burgers or fish?'

'I really don't mind.'

'You're the guest. You choose.'

'All right. Fish.'

She yelled to her husband: 'Dale! He wants fish.'

Dale came in from the garden. 'Fish. Great idea. Do you want to drive or shall I?'

'Drive where?'

'To get the fish.'

'I'm happy to drive.'

But when we got in the car he said, 'Okay, head along the beach.'

'What, drive on the beach?'

'Yeah. It's good to drive on the beach.'

'Where are we going?'

'You want fish?'

'I thought we were going to the mini-mart or somewhere.'

'You're going to have the best fish you ever tasted.'

The wind was whipping the sand up. The ocean waves were still a way off, but the noise was like distant thunder. Dale stopped at a hut to pick up a net, then said, 'Okay. Now go that way about four miles.'

'What!'

'You can put your foot down.'

I wasn't sure about this. The beach was huge and flat and stretched far away in either direction. I said, 'You know what? I'm pretty sure I'm not insured for driving on the beach. This is a hire car.'

He looked at me sadly. 'Maybe it's time to live a little?'

He was probably right. I put my foot down as instructed and whizzed along the sands. No traffic, no white lines, nobody. Dale turned the Muddy Waters CD up loud and started headbanging. We were rocking along with spray hitting the windscreen when he shouted, 'Stop!'

I hit the brakes and we skidded to a halt.

'Take your trousers off.'

'I beg your pardon?' I wished I'd chosen burgers.

'I can see them.'

'See what?'

'The fish. Take your trousers off.'

I took my trousers off as instructed and Dale got the net out. He took one side and handed the other to me and we walked down to the water's edge, then waded out into the waves until we were waist deep. The water was roaring around us. Spray soaked me. Dale waved at me to pull the net taut. Then he stood and waited, and watched. 'When I call, run like hell for the shore.'

I had a growing fear that sharks were going to be involved in this somewhere. But I held on to the net and waited until he shouted 'Now!' and then we both ran as fast as we could to the shore, dragging the net with us.

I fell onto the sand, and saw, struggling to escape the mesh, three or four big mullet.

Dale bashed them on the head, bagged them and chucked them in the back of the car. 'Let's pick up some mussels for a starter.'

A feast. We went back to the house and ate outside, gorging ourselves on barbecued fish, watching the sun set into the ocean. They asked where I was heading next and I told them I didn't know.

'If you want to go somewhere important to the Maori,' said Dale, 'you should go to Cape Reinga.'

He showed me on the map. It was the most northerly tip of the North Island. 'It's a place of huge spiritual importance.'

'What's special about it?'

'It's the end of the road.'

'I've heard that before.'

'No, this really is the end of the road.'

The next morning I continued up the coast to Kaitaia. I stopped to fill up with fuel and as I went to lift the pump off the cradle a voice yelled 'No you don't!' and out of the garage came an old boy in grey overalls and baseball cap who immediately reminded me of Mr Goodall from the garage way back when.

He handled the pump with a swagger, one hand on the trigger, the other on the car roof.

'Your vehicle's pretty mucky.'

'I've driven a long way.'

'I had a Holden once. It was hard work.'

'It's just a hire car.' I hadn't even known what make it was.

A big gull flew overhead. An old sign squeaked in the wind.

'You know what I heard?' he said. 'They've come up with a car that you don't have to drive. You just get in it, call out your coordinates to the satnav and it takes you right there.'

'I heard that, it was on the radio.'

'There'll be no more accidents. No more traffic jams. If there's trouble ahead the on-board computer will just plot another route.'

'Fantastic.'

'The driver can just sit back, or do some work, or watch a film.'

'Or have a sandwich.'

'You're right. He could have a sandwich.'

We both thought about the idea in silence for a minute.

'Car like that wouldn't catch on round here though,' he said.

The pump clicked. He shook the last few drops out of the nozzle. 'Where you headed?'

'Cape Reinga.'

He nodded, knowingly. 'Right at the lights and just keep on driving, 'til you can't drive any more.'

I continued ever north on a long, straight road, heading out on a finger of land, coastline on both sides now. No traffic, just wild beaches and wilder winds, the earth red-raw from the battering.

Finally I reached the lighthouse on the cape, and there was the Tasman Sea colliding violently with the Pacific. Nothing beyond but a pale horizon.

The cape is sacred to the Maori because it's the entrance to the underworld. They call it *Te Rerenga Wairua*, which means 'the jumping off place of spirits'. According to mythology, this is where the dead leave *Aotearoa* (New Zealand) and travel back to their homeland, *Hawaiiki*. They leap from the ancient pohutukawa tree which clings to the headland below the lighthouse.

I stood as close to the cliff edge as I dared. The earth just stopped and the drop was sheer, and yet, despite the hostile seas below and the bare rock, it didn't feel threatening. It was a place of renewal, a place so elemental it made you feel weightless. For a moment it was as if I was in the air, hanging, like one of the gulls.

This really was the end of the road, and the fact that I'd got there in a hire car didn't diminish the experience one bit.

I took some pictures. Then turned my Holden around and, with Sonny Boy Williamson on the stereo, headed back on the long journey home.